5-INGREDIENT
MEDITERRANEAN
COOKBOOK

5-INGREDIENT
MEDITERRANEAN
COOKBOOK

101 Easy and Flavorful Recipes
for Every Day

DENISE HAZIME

PHOTOGRAPHY BY ANNIE MARTIN

ROCKRIDGE
PRESS

Interior and Cover Designer: Lisa Forde
Art Producer: Michael Hardgrove
Editor: Daniel Edward Petrino
Production Editor: Andrew Yackira
Photography © 2019 Annie Martin. Food styling by Craig Murli.
Author photo courtesy of © Leah Hardy Photography

ISBN: Print 978-1-64611-125-1
eBook 978-1-64611-126-8

Ro

To my amazing girls,
London and Berlin,
I love you and I hope I make you proud.

And to my husband, Crisantos,
who had to endure a few drama-filled
moments while I wrote this book—
I love you!

Contents

Introduction

Some of my first memories as a child are of looking out to the deep blue Mediterranean Sea, inhaling the smell of the saltwater, and feeling the sun and humidity on my skin. I would jump into the sea and play all day on the golden sand. Afterward I'd enjoy a dinner of kebabs, spiced rice, salads topped with feta cheese, bowls of hummus, and fresh bread. When I was a child, my parents, who are of Lebanese descent, would take our family on trips to Lebanon, Italy, and all over the Mediterranean coast. We'd walk through the markets, eat authentic street food or dine at a favorite local restaurant, and relax while people-watching. Eating great food wasn't a treat only while traveling; it was part of our everyday lives. At family gatherings, celebrations, funerals, and weddings, food was almost always a focal point of the event. It's an integral part of the Mediterranean culture and heritage.

The amazing thing about the cuisine of the Mediterranean region is that while it differs from village to village and city to city, the basics of the cuisine remain constant. Living in America, it's hard to differentiate what food is authentic and what has been "Americanized." While there are a lot of great authentic and fusion restaurants, their version of Mediterranean cuisine fuses with local flavors, changing the experience for the American diner. However, with the wealth of information now at our fingertips, it's easy to research and determine the authenticity of the dishes being served.

While many people want to prepare the healthy dishes that the Mediterranean region is known for, it's easy to get overwhelmed by recipes that we see on TV or read online. Sometimes we see something that looks tasty, but the recipe looks too complicated to prepare at home. I'm a working mom with a thousand activities and to-do lists going at once, but I always try to make homemade meals for my family at least five days a week. I've embraced the KISS rule: keep it simple, stupid. And this book allows you to do that. In general, Mediterranean cuisine is not very complicated, and this book provides recipes that embrace that rule. Most of the recipes in this book have five main ingredients, with a few extra staple ingredients common to Mediterranean cooking that you most likely already keep in your fridge or pantry. The main ingredients should also be readily available at most grocery stores so that even shopping isn't stressful.

Flavors of the Mediterranean

What do you think of when you hear the word *Mediterranean*? Deep blue waters? Beautiful historical structures? Shimmering sandy beaches? If so, then you are correct. But the Mediterranean also alludes to a collection of countries that share many commonalities in culture, tradition, and, best of all, food. The ingredients in Mediterranean dishes are known to be fresh, bold in flavor, balanced in sweetness or acidity, and assembled a thousand different ways.

The countries of the Mediterranean are known to have warm, dry climates in the summer and mild, cool winters. While the topography can differ in each region, with some countries having large mountain ranges and others having vast deserts, almost all of the countries that border the Mediterranean Sea can brag about golden beaches. All of this nice weather and scenery lends itself to a very active lifestyle for the inhabitants of these countries. And, since these countries border the Mediterranean Sea, they rely on the sea for a lot of resources, like seafood and salt.

There are quite a few ingredients that are very common in the majority of recipes that contribute to the robust flavors of the region. The following ingredients should be staples in your pantry or refrigerator if you're planning on pursuing Mediterranean-style cooking: garlic, olive oil, onions, lemons, vinegar, pine nuts, almonds, parsley, and oregano. What taste comes to mind when you think about these ingredients? Bright, bold flavors! That's why they are so important in the cuisine of the Mediterranean, whether it's recipes from Spain, Greece, Turkey, Lebanon, or Italy.

Garlic. Garlic can have so many different characteristics and flavors. If you want a robust, pungent flavor, add raw garlic to a dish. For a sweet, mild caramelized flavor, roast the garlic bulb with a little olive oil. And for a nutty flavor, pan fry it in a little bit of oil. Garlic is so popular; it is the most common ingredient in recipes from Mediterranean countries.

Olive Oil. This is the true base to every meal. If you look across the Mediterranean, almost every country has a system of producing olive oil. Throughout the country-side, you'll see thousands upon thousands of olive trees with a variety of different olives that produce different flavor notes in the olive oil. So, the oil's flavor depends on the olive that it came from; sometimes it's a bit spicy, other times it's a bit fruity. I prefer to use extra-virgin olive oil because it is the first press of the olives without any refining or processing and has the most flavor.

Onions. These are also a staple in many dishes, and, similar to garlic, they contribute different characteristics. If eaten raw, they have a strong, robust but fresh flavor; when slowly sautéed, they are sweet and caramelized; and when cooked on high heat with some oil, they give off a nutty flavor.

Lemons and Vinegar. These two ingredients are so important to the fresh flavor the Mediterranean is known for. Their acidity helps make dishes taste fresh and bright, yet balanced. Imagine what a salad would taste like without lemon juice or vinegar. Using lemon zest can add even more flavor to any recipe.

Almonds, Pine Nuts, and Pistachios. These very common nuts are native to the region. Almonds are a nice, versatile nut that can be cut into slices or slivers. They can be toasted with some butter to finish off a dish with a crunch or used in a dish to add more substance and hearty flavor. I like to think of pine nuts as the delicate nut because their flavor is mild, and when lightly toasted, they give off a sweet note. Pine nuts are also very versatile and can be used to make a paste or dip or top a dish to give it a crunchy texture. Finally, pistachios are great when added to a dish because of their crunchy texture, bright-green color, and earthy flavor.

Parsley, Oregano, Thyme, Cilantro, Basil. These are the five most popular herbs used in Mediterranean cuisine. Parsley is commonly used to finish off a dish for some added freshness, but it's also an integral part of many recipes, especially salads. The earthy, minty notes of fresh oregano and thyme pair well with soft cheeses. When they are dried, you can add them to sauces and stews for a stronger flavor. Basil and cilantro add a fresh, slightly sweet flavor to dishes, but are also great in sauces and marinades to add a deeper flavor.

These ingredients will be your go-tos when making traditional Mediterranean recipes. You're now ready to prepare a wide variety of recipes that are simple, healthy, and full of flavor.

The Mediterranean Lifestyle

Not only is Mediterranean cuisine easy to make, it's also good for you. The regimen of eating in the Mediterranean (commonly called the Mediterranean diet) is one of the healthiest diet lifestyles. It promotes a healthy heart and reduction in occurrence of diabetes. The nutritional value of the ingredients helps increase the amount of fiber, proteins, omega-3s, antioxidants, carotenoids, and minerals in your diet. You'll notice that a lot of recipes incorporate fresh ingredients, and whole grains and beans (which are full of complex carbohydrates and protein) are widely used. Although dairy is used, the main source of fat comes from olive oil, which is one of the most heart-healthy fats. You'll also see that you can easily interchange some of the proteins (meats, poultry, dairy, and fish) or omit them entirely if desired. These recipes are meant to be versatile depending on your dietary needs.

Mediterranean cuisine has developed over thousands of years and has been enjoyed by millions of people. It has been embraced as a healthier way of eating. The Mediterranean lifestyle incorporates living off the land and whatever is currently in season. Processed foods are not a traditional part of this lifestyle; to this day, you'll find that "fast food" refers to their traditional dishes made in a portable fashion. While incorporating this type of eating into your life may seem like it's going to be more work, it doesn't have to be. This book will teach you how to make easy, nutritious recipes that can be quickly prepared any night of the week.

Braised Chicken and Mushrooms, Page 84

CHAPTER 1

Quality Over Quantity

We hear the phrase *quality over quantity* all the time, but what exactly does it mean when it comes to food? Food and calories come in many different forms and flavors, so in this book *quality over quantity* refers to the type of ingredients you are using. In the introduction, I mentioned that Mediterranean cuisine usually uses ingredients that are fresh or perishable; not many processed foods are used. This chapter will discuss what you need to keep in stock in your kitchen in order to make cooking easier and the best ways to store these ingredients.

The Mediterranean Pantry

Maintaining a pantry stocked with Mediterranean staples is so important in making your cooking life easier. If you are able to keep your kitchen stocked with these items, weekday dinners will be stress-free.

FRESH AND PERISHABLE

Garlic. A pillar of Mediterranean cooking. You will find it in so many recipes because it adds so much flavor on its own while enhancing the flavors of other food items.

Shallots. These look like a small purple onions, but have a milder flavor. Their flavor is best described as a mix of an onion and garlic blended together.

Potatoes. This starchy ingredient soaks up all the flavors of a dish while adding substance and nutrients.

SPICES

Cumin. This spice is very earthy and strong. A little goes a long way.

Coriander. This spice is the ground up seeds of the cilantro plant. It is a mild spice.

Nutmeg. This spice is also earthy but mild in flavor. It is very versatile because it can be used in both savory and sweet recipes.

Allspice. This spice has a warm flavor that is similar to cloves but not as robust.

Paprika. This spice is red and has a smoky flavor. It is sometimes labelled as smoked, Hungarian, or Spanish. The different versions are all similar in flavor and any will work for the recipes in this book.

CANNED AND JARRED GOODS

Garbanzo Beans/Chickpeas. These are a staple in Mediterranean cooking. They are small rounded beans about the size of a marble that are packed with protein and complex carbohydrates.

Tomato Sauce (plain). Tomato sauce is commonly used in many recipes. In order to control the flavor of the dish, you want to make sure that it is plain tomato sauce without any added herbs or seasoning.

Diced Tomatoes. These often come with a bit of tomato sauce in them. I like to use them when I want a bit more texture in my sauce or dish.

Olives (green and black). Olives always pack a robust flavor, and those in brine in a jar have a much better flavor than the ones in a can. I prefer to use pitted Kalamata olives.

Tahini Paste. Tahini is made up of ground sesame seeds; it can add a nutty flavor to any sauce and help thicken it as well. Its flavor is best preserved in a glass jar.

DRY GOODS

Pasta. I like to keep a variety of different shapes, sizes, and flavors of pasta stocked in my pantry. Pasta is a plain canvas that's easy to cook and adapt to many flavors using only a few ingredients.

Bulgur Wheat (#1 and #3). This is a type of cracked durum wheat. It can be prepared/cooked after being soaked. The # refers to the size of the grain; 1 is the finest and 4 is the coarsest. You will find that bulgur #1 and #3 are the most commonly used and take less time to cook.

Rice. There are several different types of rice used in this region: long grain, short grain, basmati, Bomba, and arborio. It's good to note that the different rice types cook at different times, some longer than others. All are readily available in any local grocery store.

Quinoa. This is a type of seed that is gluten-free and full of amino acids. Because it is cooked similarly to the way you cook rice or bulgur, they are easily interchange-able in recipes. Quinoa comes in a few different colors, more commonly purple or yellow.

Lentils (brown, green, red). These are actually legumes, not grains. Because red lentils tend to disintegrate when they are cooked, they are great for soups. Brown and green lentils have a firmer skin and are better at holding their shape during cooking.

How to Shop for Fruits and Vegetables

Fruits and vegetables are a big part of what makes Mediterranean cuisine so healthy. There is an abundance of fresh vegetables and fruit used in many of the recipes. Here are some tips to help you shop.

- Don't buy fruits and vegetables that are completely ripe at the store unless you plan on eating or cooking with them within one day. Buying fruits and vegetables that are not completely ripe gives them time to ripen on your countertop.

- Plan your menu ahead of shopping so you buy what you need; you won't have veggies going bad because you didn't use them.

- Buying frozen vegetables is a viable alternative to fresh. A lot of vegetables freeze well and can work in a recipe if they are going to be cooked in a sauce or a stew. For example, I wouldn't buy frozen squash because it tends to become soggy and loses its firm shape, but I would definitely buy frozen green beans, frozen peas, or frozen okra because their textures do not change when frozen, and they keep well in the freezer for a few months.

- Smell your fruits and veggies. While this applies more to fruit, it can work for vegetables as well. Most of the time, if they smell good at the store, they will have a good flavor when you cut them open. One example is cantaloupe. If you can almost taste the melon from the smell, then it will be a good pick. Another example is a tomato; If you can smell the tomato, it will have a nice sweet, acidic flavor and most likely won't be a spongy mess.

- Choose fruits and vegetables that are small and vibrant in color. The smaller ones usually have a more concentrated flavor. Colorful produce has many different phytochemicals that work to enhance the nutrients in foods.

The Fridge and Freezer

We often open the fridge and stare inside, looking for an ingredient to inspire us to cook something. With this book, as long as you have the basics in your pantry and your fridge, you should be able to whip up a healthy, satisfying dish.

THE FRIDGE

Garlic. The many attributes of garlic were previously discussed in the Fresh and Perishable section. However, a shortcut is to buy the garlic peeled and ready to go. You can buy minced garlic in a squeeze tube or even in a jar with olive oil. Just make sure that there aren't too many other ingredients added to the minced garlic.

Lemon Juice. You can juice your own lemons and store it in a jar or just buy lemon juice in a bottle ready to go. If you do buy it, make sure to buy pure lemon juice, not a mixture of citric acid and other ingredients.

Feta Cheese. This is great to have on hand because it can be stored in the fridge for a few months. It's great to throw on a salad or veggies or to add flavor to a flatbread.

Greek Yogurt. This ingredient is good to keep on hand for whipping up a side dish or dip. An unopened container can be stored in the fridge for up to 2 weeks.

Butter. This versatile ingredient can be used in so many ways, from main dishes to dessert or to finish off a dish. It is important to buy good quality butter that has a high butterfat content. And always skip the margarine.

THE FREEZER

Beef. To help with recipe planning, keep a variety of cuts and some ground beef on hand and store them in plastic bags labelled with the date. It can be taken out the night before and put it in the fridge to defrost. Doing this means you don't have to run to the butcher or grocery store before every meal.

Chicken. Buy a variety of cuts, such as a whole chicken, thighs, drumsticks, boneless breasts, and ground. These should be stored similarly to beef, in plastic bags labelled with the date. Again, this helps with recipe planning and makes it easier for you to whip up a quick dinner.

Lamb. Cuts include shoulder, shank, chops, and ground lamb. While it may not be your first choice of meat, it is very popular in Mediterranean cooking—give it a try and see how your family likes it.

Fish. Buy an assortment of fish that can store well in the freezer; the most common types of fish used are salmon, shrimp, red snapper, and sea bass. Because fish can be expensive, it's important to work it into your meal planning so you use it before it expires.

Vegetables. It's good to keep a variety of frozen vegetables on hand; green beans, okra, carrots, and peas are all frequently used. Make sure to buy organic or a reputable, quality brand.

Puff Pastry or Phyllo Dough. This is great to have on hand when you have unexpected guests coming and need to whip up an appetizer or dessert.

How to Use This Book

This book was written to help the reader put together an easy lunch or dinner in a short time period. The ingredient lists for the recipes in this book were purposefully kept short; they'll have no more than five main ingredients.

BASIC INGREDIENTS

As previously mentioned, I kept the KISS rule (keep it simple, stupid) in mind while writing the ingredient lists and the recipes. If you plan on adopting these recipes into your weekly cooking routine, there are a few basic food staples that I assume you will have stocked: garlic, onions, lemon juice, extra-virgin olive oil, salt, pepper, parsley, basil, and thyme. Each of the five main ingredients is denoted throughout the recipes with red arrows.

The ingredients in this book are ones that you should be able to find in almost any grocery store. I tried to make the ingredient lists understandable for any level of cooking ability, whether you are a professional chef, novice cook, or somewhere in between. The recipes are written in the same fashion. Nothing is so complicated that a beginner chef could not understand. Because hectic weekly schedules can make eating something healthy and nutritious seem like a daunting task, I tried to keep the recipes simple enough so that most can be prepared in under 30 minutes. The key is to plan ahead and look through the recipes, deciding what will be on your menu this week. Then make sure you have enough of the staples on hand and shop for the main ingredients to get started.

Choosing Quality Ingredients

Now that we've covered what you should have stocked in your pantry, fridge, and freezer, let's talk a little about the "free" ingredients that should be readily available and how important the quality of those ingredients can be because they are found in the majority of recipes.

An important group of ingredients to keep in mind are the herbs. These you will have to purchase weekly. Another option is to try keeping plants in your garden, so when you need some for a recipe you can just go and cut what you need.

Make sure that you use a good quality olive oil, one that is extra-virgin—that means it's the first press of the olives and has not been processed. Olive oil can contribute such great flavor to a recipe, so it's important to choose one that you like.

Salt and pepper are both basics. Try using Mediterranean sea salt instead of regular table salt; sea salt contains more minerals and less iodine. When it comes to black pepper, I like to keep ground black pepper on hand and also whole black peppercorns that I can grind up with a pepper grinder. The grinder usually gives you a coarser grind for the pepper, and for some recipes I like the pepper to stand out.

LABELS

You'll see that the recipes have different labels associated with them. These are to help you easily determine what kind of recipe it is. We all have different dietary needs, or different lifestyles, so this will help you sort the recipes faster.

Some of the labels are:

- 30 Minutes or Less

- Dairy-free

- Freezer Friendly

- Gluten-free

- Vegan

- Vegetarian

TIPS

The tips section is a great way of understanding how you can change up the recipe by adjusting it to suit your palate or avoiding ingredients you may not like.

- **Prep Tip:** How to prepare an ingredient more efficiently or methods that you can use to complete tasks ahead of time.

- **Substitution Tip:** How to replace an ingredient with an alternative.

- **Variation Tip:** How or when you can change out ingredients for other ingredients in order to suit your diet or just to try something new.

- **Storage Tip:** How to store different ingredients (broths, herbs, sauces), or how to store leftovers.

LEMONY OLIVES AND FETA MEDLEY,
PAGE 15

CHAPTER 2

Snacks and Small Plates

Sometimes small plates, appetizers, or snacks are an afterthought. But that doesn't have to be the case. Mediterranean recipes have so many flavors to work with—from sweet, to pungent, to spicy. This book focuses on quick and easy recipes that will get you excited about small plates, using ingredients like olives, dates, and different cheeses. These recipes and ingredients are a window into what the recipes from the rest of the book will look like.

Creamy Traditional Hummus

SERVES: 8 | **PREP TIME:** 5 MINUTES

Hummus is one of the most popular and versatile dishes in Mediterranean cuisine. It can be used as a dip, a spread for sandwiches, an appetizer, or even a main dish. The best part is that it can be whipped up in less than 5 minutes!

» 1 (15-ounce) can garbanzo beans, rinsed and drained

2 cloves garlic, peeled

¼ cup lemon juice

1 teaspoon salt

» ¼ cup plain Greek yogurt

» ½ cup tahini paste

2 tablespoons extra-virgin olive oil, divided

1. Add the garbanzo beans, garlic cloves, lemon juice, and salt to a food processor fitted with a chopping blade. Blend for 1 minute, until smooth.

2. Scrape down the sides of the processor. Add the Greek yogurt, tahini paste, and 1 tablespoon of olive oil and blend for another minute, until creamy and well combined.

3. Spoon the hummus into a serving bowl. Drizzle the remaining tablespoon of olive oil on top.

VARIATION TIP: When serving, garnish the hummus with cayenne pepper or paprika for a pop of color and flavor.

STORAGE TIP: Hummus can be stored in an airtight container in the fridge for up to a week.

PER SERVING: Calories: 189; Protein: 7g; Total Carbohydrates: 14g; Sugars: 2g; Fiber: 4g; Total Fat: 13g; Saturated Fat: 2g; Cholesterol: 1mg; Sodium: 313mg

Smoky Baba Ghanoush

SERVES: 6 | **PREP TIME:** 50 MINUTES | **COOK TIME:** 40 MINUTES

Baba Ghanoush works great as a side dish or a spread for sandwiches. The smoky flavor of the eggplant gives it a unique taste, while the citrus from the lemon balances the flavor.

» 2 large
eggplants, washed

¼ cup lemon juice

1 teaspoon garlic, minced

1 teaspoon salt

» ½ cup tahini paste

3 tablespoons
extra-virgin olive oil

1. Grill the whole eggplants over a low flame using a gas stovetop or grill. Rotate the eggplant every 5 minutes to make sure that all sides are cooked evenly. Continue to do this for 40 minutes.

2. Remove the eggplants from the stove or grill and put them onto a plate or into a bowl; cover with plastic wrap. Let sit for 5 to 10 minutes.

3. Using your fingers, peel away and discard the charred skin of the eggplants. Cut off the stem.

4. Put the eggplants into a food processor fitted with a chopping blade. Add the lemon juice, garlic, salt, and tahini paste, and pulse the mixture 5 to 7 times.

5. Pour the eggplant mixture onto a serving plate. Drizzle with the olive oil. Serve chilled or at room temperature.

VARIATION TIP: To make the dip more colorful, garnish with freshly chopped parsley and pomegranate seeds.

STORAGE TIP: Baba ghanoush can be stored in an airtight container for up to 1 week in the fridge.

PER SERVING: Calories: 230; Protein: 5g;
Total Carbohydrates: 16g; Sugars: 7g; Fiber: 7g;
Total Fat: 18g; Saturated Fat: 3g; Cholesterol: 0mg;
Sodium: 416mg

Creamy Tzatziki

SERVES: 6 | **PREP TIME:** 10 MINUTES

Tzatziki is one of the great dips and sauces of the Mediterranean. Almost every country has a version of this. Some contain dill; others mint. It's so versatile because it can be a dip, topping, or spread for many different foods.

» 2 Persian cucumbers

» 3 cups Greek yogurt

2 medium garlic cloves, minced

½ teaspoon salt

» 1 teaspoon dried dill or mint

1. Cut off both tips of the cucumber. Using a vegetable grater, grate the cucumber onto a paper towel. Alternatively, finely chop the cucumbers.

2. Wrap the towel around the cucumbers and squeeze out the excess liquid.

3. Put the prepared cucumbers into a large bowl and add the Greek yogurt, garlic, and salt. Stir until well combined.

4. Add the mint or dill and stir.

PREP TIP: You can make this a day ahead and store it in the fridge, which will take some sharpness off the garlic and allow the flavors to infuse. When you are ready to serve, drizzle some olive oil over the top for added color and flavor.

PER SERVING: Calories: 127; Protein: 11g; Total Carbohydrates: 7g; Sugars: 5g; Fiber: 1g; Total Fat: 6g; Saturated Fat: 3g; Cholesterol: 16mg; Sodium: 237mg

Lemony Olives and Feta Medley

SERVES: 8 | **PREP TIME:** 10 MINUTES

What's more Mediterranean than olives and feta cheese? This quick dish brings together two of the most popular ingredients from the region with a burst of fresh flavors.

» 1 (1-pound) block of Greek feta cheese

» 3 cups mixed olives (Kalamata and green), drained from brine; pitted preferred

¼ cup extra-virgin olive oil

3 tablespoons lemon juice

» 1 teaspoon grated lemon zest

» 1 teaspoon dried oregano

» Pita bread, for serving

1. Cut the feta cheese into ½-inch squares and put them into a large bowl.

2. Add the olives to the feta and set aside.

3. In a small bowl, whisk together the olive oil, lemon juice, lemon zest, and oregano.

4. Pour the dressing over the feta cheese and olives and gently toss together to evenly coat everything.

5. Serve with pita bread.

VARIATION TIP: For a kick of spice, add ½ teaspoon red pepper flakes to the dressing. And, instead of serving in a bowl, you can serve the olives and cheese on skewers, adding cherry tomatoes between the olives and cheese.

PER SERVING: Calories: 406; Protein: 8g; Total Carbohydrates: 8g; Sugars: 2g; Fiber: 0g; Total Fat: 38g; Saturated Fat: 12g; Cholesterol: 51mg; Sodium: 1,658mg

Zesty Artichoke Antipasto

SERVES: 4 | **PREP TIME:** 10 MINUTES

This is a quick antipasto dish that can be whipped up in a pinch. It includes a variety of vegetables with an array of flavors, such as smoky red peppers and tangy olives.

» 1 (12-ounce) jar roasted red peppers, drained, stemmed, and seeded

» 8 artichoke hearts, either frozen (thawed), or jarred (drained)

» 1 (16-ounce) can garbanzo beans, drained

» 1 cup whole Kalamata olives, drained

» ¼ cup balsamic vinegar

½ teaspoon salt

1. Cut the peppers into ½-inch slices and put them into a large bowl.

2. Cut the artichoke hearts into quarters, and add them to the bowl.

3. Add the garbanzo beans, olives, balsamic vinegar, and salt.

4. Toss all the ingredients together. Serve chilled.

VARIATION TIP: To add a pop of fresh flavor, add 3 tablespoons freshly chopped parsley or basil. To add some extra heat, add ½ teaspoon red pepper flakes.

PER SERVING: Calories: 281; Protein: 7g; Total Carbohydrates: 30g; Sugars: 3g; Fiber: 10g; Total Fat: 15g; Saturated Fat: 2g; Cholesterol: 0mg; Sodium: 1,237mg

Quick Garlic Mushrooms

SERVES: 4 TO 6 | **PREP TIME:** 10 MINUTES | **COOK TIME:** 10 MINUTES

Mushrooms on their own can be dull to eat, but a bit of garlic, butter, and fresh herbs take this dish from bland to bam in minutes.

» 2 pounds cremini mushrooms, cleaned

» 3 tablespoons unsalted butter

2 tablespoons garlic, minced

½ teaspoon salt

½ teaspoon freshly ground black pepper

1. Cut each mushroom in half, stem to top, and put them into a bowl.

2. Preheat a large sauté pan or skillet over medium heat.

3. Cook the butter and garlic in the pan for 2 minutes, stirring occasionally.

4. Add the mushrooms and salt to the pan and toss together with the garlic butter mixture. Cook for 7 to 8 minutes, stirring every 2 minutes.

5. Remove the mushrooms from the pan and pour into a serving dish. Top with black pepper.

VARIATION TIP: For a pop of color, top the mushrooms with freshly chopped parsley or chives. These mushrooms also make a great topping for pasta, pizza, or mashed potatoes.

PER SERVING: Calories: 183; Protein: 9g; Total Carbohydrates: 10g; Sugars: 3g; Fiber: 3g; Total Fat: 9g; Saturated Fat: 5g; Cholesterol: 23mg; Sodium: 334mg

Cheesy Dates

SERVES: 12 TO 15 | **PREP TIME:** 15 MINUTES | **COOK TIME:** 10 MINUTES

This is an easy way to turn plain dates into a tasty appetizer or dessert. This dish can be made in advance and stored in the fridge until serving time.

» 1 cup pecans, shells removed

» 1 (8-ounce) container mascarpone cheese

» 20 medjool dates

1. Preheat the oven to 350°F. Put the pecans on a baking sheet and bake for 5 to 6 minutes, until lightly toasted and aromatic. Take the pecans out of the oven and let cool for 5 minutes.

2. Once cooled, put the pecans in a food processor fitted with a chopping blade and chop until they resemble the texture of bulgur wheat or coarse sugar.

3. Reserve ¼ cup of ground pecans in a small bowl. Pour the remaining chopped pecans into a larger bowl and add the mascarpone cheese.

4. Using a spatula, mix the cheese with the pecans until evenly combined.

5. Spoon the cheese mixture into a piping bag.

6. Using a knife, cut one side of the date lengthwise, from the stem to the bottom. Gently open and remove the pit.

7. Using the piping bag, squeeze a generous amount of the cheese mixture into the date where the pit used to be. Close up the date and repeat with the remaining dates.

8. Dip any exposed cheese from the stuffed dates into the reserved chopped pecans to cover it up.

9. Set the dates on a serving plate; serve immediately or chill in the fridge until you are ready to serve.

VARIATION TIP: After filling the dates, wrap them in prosciutto and then serve.

PER SERVING: Calories: 253; Protein: 2g; Total Carbohydrates: 31g; Sugars: 27g; Fiber: 4g; Total Fat: 15g; Saturated Fat: 4g; Cholesterol: 27mg; Sodium: 7mg

Oven-Roasted Balsamic Beets

SERVES: 8 TO 10 | **PREP TIME:** 20 MINUTES | **COOK TIME:** 40 MINUTES

I love beets. However, I didn't start loving beets until I was an adult and was served roasted beets for the first time. Roasting beets imparts a more earthy flavor than canned sweet beets have. Even if you've never liked beets before, try them this way.

» 10 medium fresh beets

4 tablespoons extra-virgin olive oil, divided

1 teaspoon salt

3 teaspoons fresh thyme leaves, stems removed

» ⅓ cup balsamic vinegar

½ teaspoon freshly ground black pepper

1. Preheat the oven to 400°F.

2. Cut off the stems and roots of the beets. Wash the beets thoroughly and dry them with a paper towel.

3. Peel the beets using a vegetable peeler. Cut the beets into ½-inch pieces and put them into a large bowl.

4. Add 2 tablespoons of olive oil, the salt, and thyme to the bowl. Toss together and pour out onto a baking sheet. Spread the beets so that they are evenly distributed.

5. Bake for 35 to 40 minutes, turning once or twice with a spatula, until the beets are tender.

6. When the beets are done cooking, set them aside and let cool for 10 minutes.

7. In a small bowl, whisk together the remaining olive oil, vinegar, and black pepper.

8. Transfer the beets into a serving bowl, spoon the vinegar mixture over the beets, and serve.

VARIATION TIP: Top with crumbled feta cheese or goat cheese. If you like more herb flavoring in your dressing, add 1 teaspoon dried oregano to the dressing when whisking.

PER SERVING: Calories: 111; Protein: 2g; Total Carbohydrates: 11g; Sugars: 7g; Fiber: 3g; Total Fat: 7g; Saturated Fat: 1g; Cholesterol: 0mg; Sodium: 374mg

Spicy Roasted Potatoes

SERVES: 5 | **PREP TIME:** 20 MINUTES | **COOK TIME:** 25 MINUTES

This is the ultimate Mediterranean potato side dish—it's so good, you may need to make a second batch before you finish eating the first! Even better, there's no peeling involved.

» 1½ pounds red potatoes or gold potatoes

3 tablespoons garlic, minced

1½ teaspoons salt

¼ cup extra-virgin olive oil

» ½ cup fresh cilantro, chopped

½ teaspoon freshly ground black pepper

» ¼ teaspoon cayenne pepper

3 tablespoons lemon juice

1. Preheat the oven to 450°F.

2. Scrub the potatoes and pat dry.

3. Cut the potatoes into ½-inch pieces and put them into a bowl.

4. Add the garlic, salt, and olive oil and toss everything together to evenly coat.

5. Pour the potato mixture onto a baking sheet, spread the potatoes out evenly, and put them into the oven, roasting for 25 minutes. Halfway through roasting, turn the potatoes with a spatula; continue roasting for the remainder of time until the potato edges start to brown.

6. Remove the potatoes from the oven and let them cool on the baking sheet for 5 minutes.

7. Using a spatula, remove the potatoes from the pan and put them into a bowl.

8. Add the cilantro, black pepper, cayenne, and lemon juice to the potatoes and toss until well mixed.

9. Serve warm.

SUBSTITUTION TIP: Cilantro can be substituted with fresh basil or parsley.

PER SERVING: Calories: 203; Protein: 3g; Total Carbohydrates: 24g; Sugars: 3g; Fiber: 3g; Total Fat: 11g; Saturated Fat: 2g; Cholesterol: 0mg; Sodium: 728mg

Bite-Size Stuffed Peppers

SERVES: 8 TO 10 | **PREP TIME:** 15 MINUTES | **COOK TIME:** 10 MINUTES

These little peppers are a healthy Mediterranean version of fried jalapeño peppers. They are full of flavor and a great finger food for any type of party or dinner.

» 20 to 25 mini sweet bell peppers, assortment of colors

1 tablespoon extra-virgin olive oil

» 4 ounces goat cheese, at room temperature

» 4 ounces mascarpone cheese, at room temperature

» 1 tablespoon fresh chives, chopped

» 1 tablespoon lemon zest

1. Preheat the oven to 400°F.

2. Remove the stem, cap, and any seeds from the peppers. Put them into a bowl and toss to coat with the olive oil.

3. Put the peppers onto a baking sheet; bake for 8 minutes.

4. Remove the peppers from the oven and let cool completely.

5. In a medium bowl, add the goat cheese, mascarpone cheese, chives, and lemon zest. Stir to combine, then spoon mixture into a piping bag.

6. Fill each pepper to the top with the cheese mixture, using the piping bag.

7. Chill the peppers in the fridge for at least 30 minutes before serving.

VARIATION TIP: Make sure you taste the filling before piping it into the peppers. Depending on how salty your goat cheese is, you may want to add ½ teaspoon of salt.

SUBSTITUTION TIP: You can replace the chives with parsley or basil if desired.

PER SERVING: Calories: 141; Protein: 4g; Total Carbohydrates: 6g; Sugars: 3g; Fiber: 2g; Total Fat: 11g; Saturated Fat: 5g; Cholesterol: 38mg; Sodium: 73mg

Fresh Gazpacho Soup, Page 30

CHAPTER 3

Soups and Salads

In this chapter, I try to show off uncommon ingredients that taste great and are healthy for you. Soups and salads are a great way to get more vegetables into your diet—but you don't want them to be boring! With these recipes, you'll find that soups and salads can be more than just starters—cold soups, lentil salads, beans, cheese, and more can be filling enough for a meal.

Easy Greek Salad

SERVES: 4 TO 6 | **PREP TIME:** 10 MINUTES

This salad is popular all over the world; you'll find variations of it in almost every type of restaurant—not just Greek restaurants. It's easy to make, and there are so many ways to customize it to your personal tastes.

» 1 head iceberg lettuce

» 1 pint (2 cups) cherry tomatoes

» 1 large cucumber

1 medium onion

½ cup extra-virgin olive oil

¼ cup lemon juice

1 teaspoon salt

1 clove garlic, minced

» 1 cup Kalamata olives, pitted

» 1 (6-ounce) package feta cheese, crumbled

1. Cut the lettuce into 1-inch pieces and put them in a large salad bowl.

2. Cut the tomatoes in half and add them to the salad bowl.

3. Slice the cucumber into bite-size pieces and add them to the salad bowl.

4. Thinly slice the onion and add it to the salad bowl.

5. In another small bowl, whisk together the olive oil, lemon juice, salt, and garlic. Pour the dressing over the salad and gently toss to evenly coat.

6. Top the salad with the Kalamata olives and feta cheese and serve.

VARIATION TIP: Try adding pepperoncini and cooked beets to this salad for even more flavor. For more protein, top the salad with grilled shrimp or chicken.

PER SERVING: Calories: 539; Protein: 9g; Total Carbohydrates: 18g; Sugars: 9g; Fiber: 4g; Total Fat: 50g; Saturated Fat: 12g; Cholesterol: 38mg; Sodium: 1,758mg

Vegan, Vegetarian, 30 Minutes or Less, Dairy-free, Gluten-free

Citrusy Spinach Salad

SERVES: 4 | **PREP TIME:** 10 MINUTES | **COOK TIME:** 5 MINUTES

The citrus dressing, and toasted pine nuts added for a variation, complement the tender, slightly sweet baby spinach in this quick and easy salad.

» 1 large ripe tomato

» 1 medium red onion

» ½ teaspoon fresh lemon zest

» 3 tablespoons balsamic vinegar

¼ cup extra-virgin olive oil

½ teaspoon salt

» 1 pound baby spinach, washed, stems removed

1. Dice the tomato into ¼-inch pieces and slice the onion into long slivers.

2. In a small bowl, whisk together the lemon zest, balsamic vinegar, olive oil, and salt.

3. Put the spinach, tomatoes, and onions in a large bowl. Pour the dressing over the salad and lightly toss to coat.

PREPARATION TIP: Spinach can wilt very quickly, so it's best to dress the salad right before serving.

VARIATION TIP: For a crunchy topping, add ⅓ cup of toasted pine nuts. Simply toast the pine nuts in a small skillet over medium-low heat for about 3 minutes, until they're golden brown.

PER SERVING: Calories: 172; Protein: 4g; Total Carbohydrates: 10g; Sugars: 2g; Fiber: 4g; Total Fat: 14g; Saturated Fat: 2g; Cholesterol: 0mg; Sodium: 389mg

Classic Tabouli

SERVES: 8 TO 10 | **PREP TIME:** 30 MINUTES

Tabouli is a traditional salad that's recently grown in popularity. This hearty salad's combination of vegetables, bulgur, and citrus dressing is sure to wake up your taste buds!

» 1 cup bulgur wheat, grind #1

4 cups Italian parsley, finely chopped

» 2 cups ripe tomato, finely diced

» 1 cup green onion, finely chopped

½ cup lemon juice

½ cup extra-virgin olive oil

1½ teaspoons salt

» 1 teaspoon dried mint

1. Before you chop the vegetables, put the bulgur in a small bowl. Rinse with water, drain, and let stand in the bowl while you prepare the other ingredients.

2. Put the parsley, tomatoes, green onion, and bulgur into a large bowl.

3. In a small bowl, whisk together the lemon juice, olive oil, salt, and mint.

4. Pour the dressing over the tomato, onion, and bulgur mixture, tossing everything together. Add additional salt to taste. Serve immediately or store in the fridge for up to 2 days.

VARIATION TIP: Try adding ¼ teaspoon cayenne pepper to give the salad a little kick.

PER SERVING: Calories: 207; Protein: 4g; Total Carbohydrates: 20g; Sugars: 1g; Fiber: 5g; Total Fat: 14g; Saturated Fat: 2g; Cholesterol: 0mg; Sodium: 462mg

Vegetarian, Gluten-free

Summer Beet Salad

SERVES: 4 TO 6 | **PREP TIME:** 20 MINUTES | **COOK TIME:** 40 MINUTES

This layered salad is great for a summertime barbecue or get-together. The sweet, earthy flavor of the beets combines with the peppery flavor of the radicchio and tangy feta cheese to awaken your taste buds.

» 6 medium to large fresh red or yellow beets

⅓ cup plus 1 tablespoon extra-virgin olive oil, divided

» 4 heads of Treviso radicchio

» 2 shallots, peeled and sliced

¼ cup lemon juice

½ teaspoon salt

» 6 ounces feta cheese, crumbled

1. Preheat the oven to 400°F.

2. Cut off the stems and roots of the beets. Wash the beets thoroughly and dry them off with a paper towel.

3. Peel the beets using a vegetable peeler. Cut into ½-inch pieces and put them into a large bowl.

4. Add 1 tablespoon of olive oil to the bowl and toss to coat, then pour the beets out onto a baking sheet. Spread the beets so that they are evenly distributed.

5. Bake for 35 to 40 minutes until the beets are tender, turning once or twice with a spatula.

6. When the beets are done cooking, set them aside and let cool for 10 minutes.

7. While the beets are cooling, cut the radicchio into 1-inch pieces and place on a serving dish.

8. Once the beets have cooled, spoon them over the radicchio, then evenly distribute the shallots over the beets.

9. In a small bowl, whisk together the remaining ⅓ cup of olive oil, lemon juice, and salt. Drizzle the layered salad with dressing. Finish off the salad with feta cheese on top.

PREP TIP: You can cook the beets ahead of time and assemble the salad when you are ready to serve.

VARIATION TIP: For a more earthy dressing, add ½ teaspoon oregano.

PER SERVING: Calories: 389; Protein: 10g; Total Carbohydrates: 22g; Sugars: 13g; Fiber: 5g; Total Fat: 31g; Saturated Fat: 9g; Cholesterol: 38mg; Sodium: 893mg

Tossed Lentil Salad with Feta Cheese

SERVES: 4 | **PREP TIME:** 10 MINUTES | **COOK TIME:** 30 MINUTES

It's not very often that you find lentils in a salad, but this recipe does it in the most perfect way. This dish brings together the mild, earthy flavor of the lentils, the sweet acidity of tomatoes, crunchy cucumbers, and tangy feta cheese.

3 cups water

» 1 cup brown or green lentils, picked over and rinsed

1½ teaspoons salt, divided

» 2 large ripe tomatoes

» 2 Persian cucumbers

⅓ cup lemon juice

½ cup extra-virgin olive oil

» 1 cup crumbled feta cheese

1. In a large pot over medium heat, bring the water, lentils, and 1 teaspoon of salt to a simmer, then reduce heat to low. Cover the pot and continue to cook, stirring occasionally, for 30 minutes. (The lentils should be cooked so that they no longer have a crunch, but still hold their form. You should be able to smoosh the lentil between your two fingers when pinched.)

2. Once the lentils are done cooking, strain them to remove any excess water and put them into a large bowl. Let cool.

3. Dice the tomatoes and cucumbers, then add them to the lentils.

4. In a small bowl, whisk together the lemon juice, olive oil, and remaining ½ teaspoon salt.

5. Pour the dressing over the lentils and vegetables. Add the feta cheese to the bowl, and gently toss all of the ingredients together.

VARIATION TIP: Fresh or dried herbs can add an earthy flavor to any dressing. For this salad, I sometimes like to add ½ teaspoon dried oregano to the dressing and garnish with freshly chopped basil.

STORAGE TIP: Store this salad in the fridge for up to 3 days.

PER SERVING: Calories: 521; Protein: 18g; Total Carbohydrates: 35g; Sugars: 4g; Fiber: 15g; Total Fat: 36g; Saturated Fat: 9g; Cholesterol: 33mg; Sodium: 1,304mg

Vegan, Vegetarian, Dairy-free, Gluten-free

Mediterranean Quinoa and Garbanzo Salad

SERVES: 8 | **PREP TIME:** 10 MINUTES | **COOK TIME:** 30 MINUTES

This protein-packed salad is easy to put together and full of flavor. Although not specific to any country, it pulls together the ingredients and flavors used across the Mediterranean region. The quinoa can be cooked in advance to save time, enabling you to assemble the dish when you're ready to serve it.

4 cups water

» 2 cups red or yellow quinoa

2 teaspoons salt, divided

1 cup thinly sliced onions (red or white)

» 1 (16-ounce) can garbanzo beans, rinsed and drained

⅓ cup extra-virgin olive oil

¼ cup lemon juice

1 teaspoon freshly ground black pepper

1. In a 3-quart pot over medium heat, bring the water to a boil.

2. Add the quinoa and 1 teaspoon of salt to the pot. Stir, cover, and let cook over low heat for 15 to 20 minutes.

3. Turn off the heat, fluff the quinoa with a fork, cover again, and let stand for 5 to 10 more minutes.

4. Put the cooked quinoa, onions, and garbanzo beans in a large bowl.

5. In a separate small bowl, whisk together the olive oil, lemon juice, remaining 1 teaspoon of salt, and black pepper.

6. Add the dressing to the quinoa mixture and gently toss everything together. Serve warm or cold.

VARIATION TIPS: This recipe provides a canvas to add any vegetables or herbs that you like. You can add chopped cherry tomatoes, cucumbers, fresh parsley, or basil. Or, you can turn it into a main course by topping with a protein like chicken or shrimp. For a greater burst of flavor, add any cheese that you like; feta cheese or goat cheese would work well in this salad.

STORAGE TIP: This salad also stores very well in the refrigerator, so it's great for prepping ahead of time.

PER SERVING: Calories: 318; Protein: 9g; Total Carbohydrates: 43g; Sugars: 6g; Fiber: 6g; Total Fat: 13g; Saturated Fat: 1g; Cholesterol: 0mg; Sodium: 585mg

Fresh Gazpacho Soup

SERVES: 6 TO 8 | **PREP TIME:** 15 MINUTES

Gazpacho is full of fresh flavors. Because it involves no cooking, this is one of the easiest soups to make. This soup originated in Spain, and there are many variations of it.

½ cup of water

» 2 slices of white bread, crust removed

» 2 pounds ripe tomatoes

» 1 Persian cucumber, peeled and chopped

1 clove garlic, finely chopped

⅓ cup extra-virgin olive oil, plus more for garnish

» 2 tablespoons red wine vinegar

1 teaspoon salt

½ teaspoon freshly ground black pepper

1. Soak the bread in the water for 5 minutes; discard water when done.

2. Blend the bread, tomatoes, cucumber, garlic, olive oil, vinegar, salt, and black pepper in a food processor or blender until completely smooth.

3. Pour the soup into a glass container and store in the fridge until completely chilled.

4. When you are ready to serve, pour the soup into a bowl and top with a drizzle of olive oil.

VARIATION TIP: You can also serve the soup topped with fresh herbs, such as basil, parsley, or thyme. I also like to add half an onion or a green or red bell pepper for a little sweetness. Add these variations when blending the other ingredients.

PER SERVING: Calories: 163; Protein: 2g; Total Carbohydrates: 12g; Sugars: 1g; Fiber: 2g; Total Fat: 13g; Saturated Fat: 2g; Cholesterol: 0mg; Sodium: 442mg

Vegan, Vegetarian, Dairy-free, Freezer Friendly, Gluten-free

Easy Brown Lentil Soup

SERVES: 6 TO 8 | **PREP TIME:** 25 MINUTES | **COOK TIME:** 1 HOUR 20 MINUTES

This is a very hearty, comforting soup for a cold winter day. Not only is this soup served warm, but the spices and flavors from this soup are warmly flavorful but not spicy.

10 cups water

» 2 cups brown lentils, picked over and rinsed

2 teaspoons salt, divided

» ¼ cup long-grain rice, rinsed

3 tablespoons extra-virgin olive oil

1 large onion, chopped

» 2 medium potatoes, peeled

» 1 teaspoon ground cumin

½ teaspoon freshly ground black pepper

1. In a large pot over medium heat, bring the water, lentils, and 1 teaspoon of salt to a simmer and continue to cook, stirring occasionally, for 30 minutes.

2. At the 30-minute mark, add the rice to the lentils. Cover and continue to simmer, stirring occasionally, for another 30 minutes.

3. Remove the pot from the heat and, using a handheld immersion blender, blend the lentils and rice for 1 to 2 minutes until smooth.

4. Return the pot to the stove over low heat.

5. In a small skillet over medium heat, cook the olive oil and onions for 5 minutes until the onions are golden brown. Add the onions to the soup.

6. Cut the potatoes into ¼-inch pieces and add them to the soup.

7. Add remaining 1 teaspoon of salt, cumin, and black pepper to the soup. Stir and continue to cook for 10 to 15 minutes, or until potatoes are thoroughly cooked. Serve warm.

VARIATION TIP: When serving, garnish the bowl with a sprinkle of fresh chopped parsley. You can easily make this delicious soup even heartier by adding cooked mini meatballs and chopped carrots.

PER SERVING: Calories: 348; Protein: 18g; Total Carbohydrates: 53g; Sugars: 4g; Fiber: 20g; Total Fat: 9g; Saturated Fat: 1g; Cholesterol: 0mg; Sodium: 795mg

Quick White Bean and Vegetable Soup

SERVES: 6 | **PREP TIME:** 10 MINUTES | **COOK TIME:** 25 MINUTES

This speedy soup will deliver warm and soothing flavors in a fraction of the time it normally takes to prepare soup. The vegetables and herbs complement the hearty beans, adding even more flavor and texture.

3 tablespoons extra-virgin olive oil

1 large onion, finely chopped

3 large garlic cloves, minced

» 2 cups carrots, diced

» 2 cups celery, diced

» 2 (15-ounce) cans white beans, rinsed and drained

» 8 cups vegetable broth

1 teaspoon salt

½ teaspoon freshly ground black pepper

1. In a large pot over medium heat, cook the olive oil, onion, and garlic for 2 to 3 minutes.

2. Add the carrots and celery, and cook for another 3 to 5 minutes, stirring occasionally.

3. Add the beans, broth, salt, and pepper. Stir and let simmer for 15 to 17 minutes, stirring occasionally. Serve warm.

VARIATION TIP: I like to add a tablespoon or 2 of chopped fresh herbs, like thyme or sage, when I am sautéing the vegetables.

Also, you can add 2 cups of washed and chopped Swiss chard about 5 minutes before the soup is done simmering to make it even more hearty and flavorful. When you're ready to serve, top the soup with grated or shaved Parmesan cheese.

STORAGE TIP: Once the soup cools to room temperature, you can store the soup in the freezer in an airtight plastic container for a later date.

PER SERVING: Calories: 244; Protein: 9g; Total Carbohydrates: 36g; Sugars: 8g; Fiber: 10g; Total Fat: 7g; Saturated Fat: 1g; Cholesterol: 0mg; Sodium: 1,160mg

Vegan, Vegetarian, Dairy-free, Freezer Friendly, Gluten-free

Lemony Red Lentil Soup

SERVES: 6 TO 8 | **PREP TIME:** 10 MINUTES | **COOK TIME:** 55 MINUTES

Don't be confused by the title! Although we are using red lentils for this recipe, they'll turn an orange/yellow color and lose their shape when cooked in a soup. Red lentils have a milder flavor than green or brown lentils and are great for making a soup or stew.

» 1 cup red lentils, picked over and rinsed

» ½ cup long grain or basmati rice, rinsed

10 cups water

2 teaspoons salt

3 tablespoons extra-virgin olive oil

1 large onion, finely chopped

» 2 cups carrots, finely diced

» 1 teaspoon turmeric

» 1 lemon, cut into wedges

1. In a large pot over medium heat, heat the lentils, rice, water, and salt. Bring to a simmer for 40 minutes, stirring occasionally.

2. In a small skillet over medium-low heat, cook the olive oil and onions for 5 minutes until the onions are golden brown.

3. Add the cooked onions, carrots, and turmeric to the soup and cook for 15 minutes, stirring occasionally.

4. Serve the soup with a big squeeze of lemon over the top and a lemon wedge on the side.

PREP TIP: This soup can be made in advance; reserve the lemon until you are ready to serve.

VARIATION TIP: For a pop of color and flavor, I like to top the soup with fresh ground black pepper and freshly chopped parsley.

PER SERVING: Calories: 230; Protein: 9g; Total Carbohydrates: 37g; Sugars: 3g; Fiber: 9g; Total Fat: 8g; Saturated Fat: 1g; Cholesterol: 0mg; Sodium: 806mg

Cheesy Spinach Pies, Page 51

CHAPTER 4

Vegetables and Meatless Mains

While many restaurants are now offering vegetarian options, such as meatless hamburgers and tacos that taste like real meat, it could be said that we are moving to a vegetarian or meatless approach to diets and cooking. However, Mediterranean food has always been known for its meatless recipes that are full of bold flavor. The recipes in this chapter are as flavorful and satisfying as any dish that contains meat.

Mediterranean Veggie Bowl

SERVES: 4 | **PREP TIME:** 10 MINUTES | **COOK TIME:** 20 MINUTES

This is a great way to get a huge serving of veggies in one meal. This bowl has a rainbow of flavors and can be prepared ahead of time.

2 cups water

» 1 cup of either bulgur wheat #3 or quinoa, rinsed

1½ teaspoons salt, divided

» 1 pint (2 cups) cherry tomatoes, cut in half

» 1 large bell pepper, chopped

» 1 large cucumber, chopped

» 1 cup Kalamata olives

½ cup freshly squeezed lemon juice

1 cup extra-virgin olive oil

½ teaspoon freshly ground black pepper

1. In a medium pot over medium heat, boil the water. Add the bulgur (or quinoa) and 1 teaspoon of salt. Cover and cook for 15 to 20 minutes.

2. To arrange the veggies in your 4 bowls, visually divide each bowl into 5 sections. Place the cooked bulgur in one section. Follow with the tomatoes, bell pepper, cucumbers, and olives.

3. In a small bowl, whisk together the lemon juice, olive oil, remaining ½ teaspoon salt, and black pepper.

4. Evenly spoon the dressing over the 4 bowls.

5. Serve immediately or cover and refrigerate for later.

VARIATION TIP: Add garbanzo beans (rinsed and drained), hummus, grilled chicken, or baked fish to this dish for a boost of protein. Finish it off with freshly ground black pepper for a peppery bite.

PER SERVING: Calories: 772; Protein: 6g; Total Carbohydrates: 41g; Sugars: 3g; Fiber: 9g; Total Fat: 68g; Saturated Fat: 9g; Cholesterol: 0mg; Sodium: 1,570mg

Grilled Veggie and Hummus Wrap

SERVES: 6 | **PREP TIME:** 15 MINUTES | **COOK TIME:** 10 MINUTES

I love this wrap for a quick lunch, dinner, or party dish, especially because it can be prepared ahead of time. The layered vegetables and hummus give it tons of flavor and color.

» 1 large eggplant

1 large onion

½ cup extra-virgin olive oil

1 teaspoon salt

» 6 lavash wraps or large pita bread

» 1 cup Creamy Traditional Hummus (page 12)

1. Preheat a grill, large grill pan, or lightly oiled large skillet on medium heat.

2. Slice the eggplant and onion into circles. Brush the vegetables with olive oil and sprinkle with salt.

3. Cook the vegetables on both sides, about 3 to 4 minutes each side.

4. To make the wrap, lay the lavash or pita flat. Spread about 2 tablespoons of hummus on the wrap.

5. Evenly divide the vegetables among the wraps, layering them along one side of the wrap. Gently fold over the side of the wrap with the vegetables, tucking them in and making a tight wrap.

6. Lay the wrap seam side-down and cut in half or thirds.

7. You can also wrap each sandwich with plastic wrap to help it hold its shape and eat it later.

VARIATION TIP: You can use any vegetables that you like in this recipe; some alternatives are zucchini and bell peppers. Using a grill imparts a smoky flavor to the vegetables, so it's best to use vegetables that are easy to cook on a grill.

PER SERVING: Calories: 362; Protein: 15g; Total Carbohydrates: 28g; Sugars: 4g; Fiber: 11g; Total Fat: 26g; Saturated Fat: 3g; Cholesterol: 0mg; Sodium: 1,069mg

Spanish Green Beans

SERVES: 4 | **PREP TIME:** 10 MINUTES | **COOK TIME:** 20 MINUTES

Green beans are one of those vegetables that need some spices to excite the palate, and the addition of garlic and tomatoes does just that!

¼ cup extra-virgin olive oil

1 large onion, chopped

4 cloves garlic, finely chopped

» 1 pound green beans, fresh or frozen, trimmed

1½ teaspoons salt, divided

» 1 (15-ounce) can diced tomatoes

½ teaspoon freshly ground black pepper

1. In a large pot over medium heat, heat the olive oil, onion, and garlic; cook for 1 minute.

2. Cut the green beans into 2-inch pieces.

3. Add the green beans and 1 teaspoon of salt to the pot and toss everything together; cook for 3 minutes.

4. Add the diced tomatoes, remaining ½ teaspoon of salt, and black pepper to the pot; continue to cook for another 12 minutes, stirring occasionally.

5. Serve warm.

VARIATION TIP: For an added crunch, you can sprinkle toasted almonds or pine nuts on top when you are ready to serve. I also like to add ½ teaspoon red pepper flakes for a little spice and then finish it off with a generous squeeze of lemon.

PER SERVING: Calories: 200; Protein: 4g; Total Carbohydrates: 18g; Sugars: 9g; Fiber: 6g; Total Fat: 14g; Saturated Fat: 2g; Cholesterol: 0mg; Sodium: 844mg

Rustic Cauliflower and Carrot Hash

SERVES: 4 | **PREP TIME:** 10 MINUTES | **COOK TIME:** 10 MINUTES

This quick veggie dish is rustic and full of flavor. Serve it with pasta or rice for an even heartier dish.

3 tablespoons extra-virgin olive oil

1 large onion, chopped

1 tablespoon garlic, minced

» 2 cups carrots, diced

» 4 cups cauliflower pieces, washed

1 teaspoon salt

» ½ teaspoon ground cumin

1. In a large skillet over medium heat, cook the olive oil, onion, garlic, and carrots for 3 minutes.

2. Cut the cauliflower into 1-inch or bite-size pieces. Add the cauliflower, salt, and cumin to the skillet and toss to combine with the carrots and onions.

3. Cover and cook for 3 minutes.

4. Toss the vegetables and continue to cook uncovered for an additional 3 to 4 minutes.

5. Serve warm.

PREPARATION TIP: Buying pre-washed and pre-cut cauliflower from the grocery store will save you even more time when preparing this dish.

PER SERVING: Calories: 159; Protein: 3g; Total Carbohydrates: 15g; Sugars: 7g; Fiber: 5g; Total Fat: 11g; Saturated Fat: 2g; Cholesterol: 0mg; Sodium: 657mg

Roasted Cauliflower and Tomatoes

SERVES: 4 | **PREP TIME:** 5 MINUTES | **COOK TIME:** 25 MINUTES

This is an easy and flavorful way to dress up cauliflower. Roasting brings out the smooth, nutty flavor, which is complemented by the blistered cherry tomatoes.

» 4 cups cauliflower, cut into 1-inch pieces

6 tablespoons extra-virgin olive oil, divided

1 teaspoon salt, divided

» 4 cups cherry tomatoes

½ teaspoon freshly ground black pepper

» ½ cup grated Parmesan cheese

1. Preheat the oven to 425°F.

2. Add the cauliflower, 3 tablespoons of olive oil, and ½ teaspoon of salt to a large bowl and toss to evenly coat. Pour onto a baking sheet and spread the cauliflower out in an even layer.

3. In another large bowl, add the tomatoes, remaining 3 tablespoons of olive oil, and ½ teaspoon of salt, and toss to coat evenly. Pour onto a different baking sheet.

4. Put the sheet of cauliflower and the sheet of tomatoes in the oven to roast for 17 to 20 minutes until the cauliflower is lightly browned and tomatoes are plump.

5. Using a spatula, spoon the cauliflower into a serving dish, and top with tomatoes, black pepper, and Parmesan cheese. Serve warm.

VARIATION TIP: Try adding chopped fresh herbs like basil or parsley during the roasting to enhance the flavor of the dish. For even more flavor, the tomatoes can also be roasted with sprigs of fresh thyme or oregano.

PER SERVING: Calories: 294; Protein: 9g; Total Carbohydrates: 13g; Sugars: 6g; Fiber: 4g; Total Fat: 26g; Saturated Fat: 6g; Cholesterol: 10mg; Sodium: 858mg

Roasted Acorn Squash

SERVES: 6 | **PREP TIME:** 10 MINUTES | **COOK TIME:** 35 MINUTES

Flavorful and light, this dish is a great go-to when you want to throw something in the oven and not have to do too much. Acorn squash is not always available year-round; you can easily substitute another type of squash.

» 2 acorn squash, medium to large

2 tablespoons extra-virgin olive oil

1 teaspoon salt, plus more for seasoning

» 5 tablespoons unsalted butter

» ¼ cup chopped sage leaves

2 tablespoons fresh thyme leaves

½ teaspoon freshly ground black pepper

1. Preheat the oven to 400°F.

2. Cut the acorn squash in half lengthwise. Scrape out the seeds with a spoon and cut it horizontally into ¾-inch-thick slices.

3. In a large bowl, drizzle the squash with the olive oil, sprinkle with salt, and toss together to coat.

4. Lay the acorn squash flat on a baking sheet.

5. Put the baking sheet in the oven and bake the squash for 20 minutes. Flip squash over with a spatula and bake for another 15 minutes.

6. Melt the butter in a medium saucepan over medium heat.

7. Add the sage and thyme to the melted butter and let them cook for 30 seconds.

8. Transfer the cooked squash slices to a plate. Spoon the butter/herb mixture over the squash. Season with salt and black pepper. Serve warm.

VARIATION TIP: For a little crunch, try adding toasted pine nuts or pumpkin seeds. You can also just sprinkle some grated Parmesan onto the squash slices before serving. For a sweet note, sprinkle the squash with ¼ cup brown sugar halfway through roasting.

PER SERVING: Calories: 188; Protein: 1g; Total Carbohydrates: 16g; Sugars: 0g; Fiber: 3g; Total Fat: 15g; Saturated Fat: 7g; Cholesterol: 26mg; Sodium: 393mg

Sautéed Garlic Spinach

SERVES: 4 | **PREP TIME:** 5 MINUTES | **COOK TIME:** 10 MINUTES

The sweetness from the onions and pungent garlic work together to complement the earthy flavor of the spinach, especially when finished off with a squeeze of lemon.

¼ cup extra-virgin olive oil

1 large onion, thinly sliced

3 cloves garlic, minced

» 6 (1-pound) bags of baby spinach, washed

½ teaspoon salt

» 1 lemon, cut into wedges

1. Cook the olive oil, onion, and garlic in a large skillet for 2 minutes over medium heat.

2. Add one bag of spinach and ½ teaspoon of salt. Cover the skillet and let the spinach wilt for 30 seconds. Repeat (omitting the salt), adding 1 bag of spinach at a time.

3. Once all the spinach has been added, remove the cover and cook for 3 minutes, letting some of the moisture evaporate.

4. Serve warm with a generous squeeze of lemon over the top.

VARIATION TIP: Add grated Parmesan to the top before serving.

PER SERVING: Calories: 301; Protein: 17g; Total Carbohydrates: 29g; Sugars: 2g; Fiber: 17g; Total Fat: 14g; Saturated Fat: 2g; Cholesterol: 0mg; Sodium: 812mg

Garlicky Sautéed Zucchini with Mint

SERVES: 4 | **PREP TIME:** 5 MINUTES | **COOK TIME:** 10 MINUTES

Zucchini is a very popular vegetable along the Mediterranean because of the great year-round weather. It's very easy to grow in abundance and versatile enough to prepare in a variety of ways. You can fry it, grill it, sauté it, or even roast it.

» 3 large green zucchini

3 tablespoons extra-virgin olive oil

1 large onion, chopped

3 cloves garlic, minced

1 teaspoon salt

» 1 teaspoon dried mint

1. Cut the zucchini into ½-inch cubes.

2. In a large skillet over medium heat, cook the olive oil, onions, and garlic for 3 minutes, stirring constantly.

3. Add the zucchini and salt to the skillet and toss to combine with the onions and garlic, cooking for 5 minutes.

4. Add the mint to the skillet, tossing to combine. Cook for another 2 minutes. Serve warm.

VARIATION TIP: If you don't like mint, you can replace it with oregano.

PER SERVING: Calories: 147; Protein: 4g; Total Carbohydrates: 12g; Sugars: 6g; Fiber: 3g; Total Fat: 11g; Saturated Fat: 2g; Cholesterol: 0mg; Sodium: 607mg

Stewed Okra

SERVES: 4 | **PREP TIME:** 5 MINUTES | **COOK TIME:** 25 MINUTES

Okra can be a tricky ingredient since it can get gooey when cooked, but you don't have to worry about that with this recipe. This flavor-packed stew can be served with rice as a main dish.

¼ cup extra-virgin olive oil

1 large onion, chopped

4 cloves garlic, finely chopped

1 teaspoon salt

» 1 pound fresh or frozen okra, cleaned

» 1 (15-ounce) can plain tomato sauce

2 cups water

» ½ cup fresh cilantro, finely chopped

½ teaspoon freshly ground black pepper

1. In a large pot over medium heat, stir and cook the olive oil, onion, garlic, and salt for 1 minute.

2. Stir in the okra and cook for 3 minutes.

3. Add the tomato sauce, water, cilantro, and black pepper; stir, cover, and let cook for 15 minutes, stirring occasionally.

4. Serve warm.

STORAGE TIP: This stew freezes very well, so you can make it in advance of your meal, and you can freeze what you don't eat, saving it for when you're in need of a quick meal!

PER SERVING: Calories: 201; Protein: 4g; Total Carbohydrates: 18g; Sugars: 8g; Fiber: 6g; Total Fat: 14g; Saturated Fat: 2g; Cholesterol: 0mg; Sodium: 1,156mg

Sweet Veggie-Stuffed Peppers

SERVES: 6 | **PREP TIME:** 20 MINUTES | **COOK TIME:** 30 MINUTES

Peppers are the perfect vehicle for stuffing because of their hollow shape. They also have a sweet flavor that goes great with rice and other vegetables.

» 6 large bell peppers,
different colors

3 tablespoons
extra-virgin olive oil

1 large onion, chopped

3 cloves garlic, minced

» 1 carrot, chopped

» 1 (16-ounce) can
garbanzo beans,
rinsed and drained

» 3 cups cooked rice

1½ teaspoons salt

½ teaspoon freshly
ground black pepper

1. Preheat the oven to 350°F.

2. Make sure to choose peppers that can stand upright. Cut off the pepper cap and remove the seeds, reserving the cap for later. Stand the peppers in a baking dish.

3. In a large skillet over medium heat, cook the olive oil, onion, garlic, and carrots for 3 minutes.

4. Stir in the garbanzo beans. Cook for another 3 minutes.

5. Remove the pan from the heat and spoon the cooked ingredients to a large bowl.

6. Add the rice, salt, and pepper; toss to combine.

7. Stuff each pepper to the top and then put the pepper caps back on.

8. Cover the baking dish with aluminum foil and bake for 25 minutes.

9. Remove the foil and bake for another 5 minutes.

10. Serve warm.

VARIATION TIP: You can make this recipe even more hearty by adding ground lamb, beef, turkey, or chicken. Simply brown the meat first. Combine with the other ingredients and then continue to follow the recipe. Or add any veggies and herbs that you like: parsley, basil, peas, chopped broccoli, or celery are all good choices.

PER SERVING: Calories: 301; Protein: 8g; Total Carbohydrates: 50g; Sugars: 8g; Fiber: 8g; Total Fat: 9g; Saturated Fat: 1g; Cholesterol: 0mg; Sodium: 597mg

Moussaka

SERVES: 6 | **PREP TIME:** 55 MINUTES | **COOK TIME:** 40 MINUTES

There are many versions of Moussaka: some with meat, some vegetarian, some with a breadcrumb topping, and some with a white béchamel sauce topping. Any way that you make it, the star ingredient is the same—eggplant.

»2 large eggplants

2 teaspoons salt, divided

Olive oil spray, or olive oil for brushing

¼ cup extra-virgin olive oil

2 large onions, sliced

10 cloves garlic, sliced

»2 (15-ounce) cans diced tomatoes

»1 (16-ounce) can garbanzo beans, rinsed and drained

»1 teaspoon dried oregano

½ teaspoon freshly ground black pepper

1. Slice the eggplant horizontally into ¼-inch-thick round disks. Sprinkle the eggplant slices with 1 teaspoon of salt and place in a colander for 30 minutes. This will draw out the excess water from the eggplant.

2. Preheat the oven to 450°F. Pat the slices of eggplant dry with a paper towel and spray each side with an olive oil spray or lightly brush each side with olive oil.

3. Arrange the eggplant in a single layer on a baking sheet. Put in the oven and bake for 10 minutes. Then, using a spatula, flip the slices over and bake for another 10 minutes.

4. In a large skillet add the olive oil, onions, garlic, and remaining 1 teaspoon of salt. Cook for 3 to 5 minutes stirring occasionally. Add the tomatoes, garbanzo beans, oregano, and black pepper. Simmer for 10 to 12 minutes, stirring occasionally.

5. Using a deep casserole dish, begin to layer, starting with eggplant, then the sauce. Repeat until all ingredients have been used. Bake in the oven for 20 minutes.

6. Remove from the oven and serve warm.

VARIATION TIP: For a warm spice flavor, try adding ½ teaspoon nutmeg to the sauce. You can add a top layer by making a quick béchamel sauce and adding before you bake. Finish off the dish with fresh chopped parsley for additional flavor and color.

PER SERVING: Calories: 262; Protein: 8g; Total Carbohydrates: 35g; Sugars: 14g; Fiber: 11g; Total Fat: 11g; Saturated Fat: 1g; Cholesterol: 0mg; Sodium: 1,043mg

Vegetable-Stuffed Grape Leaves

SERVES: 6 TO 8 | **PREP TIME:** 50 MINUTES | **COOK TIME:** 45 MINUTES

Stuffed grape leaves are a very popular Mediterranean dish. Recipes vary from region to region, but each is packed with flavor! They take a bit of work to put together, but their flavor makes it all worthwhile.

» 2 cups white rice, rinsed

» 2 large tomatoes, finely diced

1 large onion, finely chopped

» 1 green onion, finely chopped

1 cup fresh Italian parsley, finely chopped

3 cloves garlic, minced

2½ teaspoons salt

½ teaspoon freshly ground black pepper

» 1 (16-ounce) jar grape leaves

1 cup lemon juice

½ cup extra-virgin olive oil

4 to 6 cups water

1. In a large bowl, combine the rice, tomatoes, onion, green onion, parsley, garlic, salt, and black pepper.

2. Drain and rinse the grape leaves.

3. Prepare a large pot by placing a layer of grape leaves on the bottom. Lay each leaf flat and trim off any stems.

4. Place 2 tablespoons of the rice mixture at the base of each leaf. Fold over the sides, then roll as tight as possible. Place the rolled grape leaves in the pot, lining up each rolled grape leaf. Continue to layer in the rolled grape leaves.

5. Gently pour the lemon juice and olive oil over the grape leaves, and add enough water to just cover the grape leaves by 1 inch.

6. Lay a heavy plate that is smaller than the opening of the pot upside down over the grape leaves. Cover the pot and cook the leaves over medium-low heat for 45 minutes. Let stand for 20 minutes before serving.

7. Serve warm or cold.

SUBSTITUTION TIP: For an added boost of protein, add a can of garbanzo beans, rinsed and drained, to the stuffing mixture.

PER SERVING: Calories: 532; Protein: 12g; Total Carbohydrates: 80g; Sugars: 9g; Fiber: 15g; Total Fat: 21g; Saturated Fat: 3g; Cholesterol: 0mg; Sodium: 995mg

Vegetarian, Gluten-free

Grilled Eggplant Rolls

SERVES: 4 TO 6 | **PREP TIME:** 30 MINUTES | **COOK TIME:** 10 MINUTES

These rolls can be made ahead of serving and stored in the fridge. The smoky flavor of the grilled eggplant combines well with the tangy cheeses.

» 2 large eggplants

1 teaspoon salt

» 4 ounces goat cheese

» 1 cup ricotta

¼ cup fresh basil, finely chopped

½ teaspoon freshly ground black pepper

Olive oil spray

1. Trim off the tops of the eggplants and cut the eggplants lengthwise into ¼-inch-thick slices. Sprinkle the slices with the salt and place the eggplant in a colander for 15 to 20 minutes. The salt will draw out excess water from the eggplant.

2. In a large bowl, combine the goat cheese, ricotta, basil, and pepper.

3. Preheat a grill, grill pan, or lightly oiled skillet on medium heat. Pat the eggplant slices dry with a paper towel and lightly spray with olive oil spray. Place the eggplant on the grill, grill pan, or skillet and cook for 3 minutes on each side.

4. Remove the eggplant from the heat and let cool for 5 minutes.

5. To roll, lay one eggplant slice flat, place a tablespoon of the cheese mixture at the base of the slice, and roll up. Serve immediately or chill until serving.

VARIATION TIP: For a punch of citrus flavor, try adding 1 teaspoon of lemon zest in the filling.

SUBSTITUTION TIP: This recipe can also be made using grilled zucchini.

PER SERVING: Calories: 255; Protein: 15g; Total Carbohydrates: 19g; Sugars: 10g; Fiber: 7g; Total Fat: 15g; Saturated Fat: 9g; Cholesterol: 44mg; Sodium: 746mg

Crispy Zucchini Fritters

SERVES: 6 | **PREP TIME:** 15 MINUTES | **COOK TIME:** 20 MINUTES

Who doesn't love fried food? These little fritters carry a punch of flavor from the garlic and herbs. Grab them while they're hot because you probably won't have any leftovers.

» 2 large green zucchinis

2 tablespoons Italian parsley, finely chopped

3 cloves garlic, minced

1 teaspoon salt

» 1 cup flour

» 1 large egg, beaten

½ cup water

» 1 teaspoon baking powder

3 cups vegetable or avocado oil

1. Grate the zucchini into a large bowl.

2. Add the parsley, garlic, salt, flour, egg, water, and baking powder to the bowl and stir to combine.

3. In a large pot or fryer over medium heat, heat oil to 365°F.

4. Drop the fritter batter into the hot oil by spoonfuls. Turn the fritters over using a slotted spoon and fry until they are golden brown, about 2 to 3 minutes.

5. Remove the fritters from the oil and drain on a plate lined with paper towels.

6. Serve warm with Creamy Tzatziki (see page 14) or Creamy Traditional Hummus (see page 12) as a dip.

VARIATION TIP: You can try adding fresh herbs like thyme, basil, or parsley to the batter.

PER SERVING: Calories: 446; Protein: 5g;
Total Carbohydrates: 19g; Sugars: 2g; Fiber: 2g;
Total Fat: 38g; Saturated Fat: 6g; Cholesterol: 31mg;
Sodium: 492mg

Cheesy Spinach Pies

SERVES: 6 TO 8 | **PREP TIME:** 20 MINUTES | **COOK TIME:** 40 MINUTES

Spinach pies are authentic Greek, Italian, and Lebanese pastries that are beloved for their creamy filling and flaky exterior. This dish has countless variations throughout the Mediterranean coast.

2 tablespoons extra-virgin olive oil

1 large onion, chopped

2 cloves garlic, minced

» 3 (1-pound) bags of baby spinach, washed

» 1 cup feta cheese

» 1 large egg, beaten

» Puff pastry sheets

1. Preheat the oven to 375°F.

2. In a large skillet over medium heat, cook the olive oil, onion, and garlic for 3 minutes.

3. Add the spinach to the skillet one bag at a time, letting it wilt in between each bag. Toss using tongs. Cook for 4 minutes. Once the spinach is cooked, drain any excess liquid from the pan.

4. In a large bowl, combine the feta cheese, egg, and cooked spinach.

5. Lay the puff pastry flat on a counter. Cut the pastry into 3-inch squares.

6. Place a tablespoon of the spinach mixture in the center of a puff-pastry square. Fold over one corner of the square to the diagonal corner, forming a triangle. Crimp the edges of the pie by pressing down with the tines of a fork to seal them together. Repeat until all squares are filled.

7. Place the pies on a parchment-lined baking sheet and bake for 25 to 30 minutes or until golden brown. Serve warm or at room temperature.

PREPARATION TIP: You can make these in advance and store in the fridge. Prior to serving, heat at 375°F for 7 minutes.

PER SERVING: Calories: 503; Protein: 16g; Total Carbohydrates: 38g; Sugars: 4g; Fiber: 6g; Total Fat: 32g; Saturated Fat: 10g; Cholesterol: 53mg; Sodium: 843mg

LEMON ORZO WITH FRESH HERBS, PAGE 56

CHAPTER 5

Rice, Grains, and Beans

Rice, grains, and beans are common dietary staples all over the world. Eighty percent of the world's population still lives on less than $3 a day, and most of the world's people would go hungry without beans, grains, and rice. The recipes in this chapter combine the basics of sustained nutrition from carbohydrates and proteins. Many of my favorite recipes come from this chapter; many of them are also meatless.

Fava and Garbanzo Bean Fūl

SERVES: 6 | **PREP TIME:** 10 MINUTES | **COOK TIME:** 10 MINUTES

Fūl is a traditional stew of mixed beans. This protein-filled recipe uses two types of beans and is topped with a lemony dressing. This versatile dish can be eaten hot or cold for breakfast, lunch, or dinner.

» 1 (16-ounce) can garbanzo beans, rinsed and drained

» 1 (15-ounce) can fava beans, rinsed and drained

3 cups water

½ cup lemon juice

3 cloves garlic, peeled and minced

1 teaspoon salt

3 tablespoons extra-virgin olive oil

1. In a 3-quart pot over medium heat, cook the garbanzo beans, fava beans, and water for 10 minutes.

2. Reserving 1 cup of the liquid from the cooked beans, drain the beans and put them in a bowl.

3. Mix the reserved liquid, lemon juice, minced garlic, and salt together and add to the beans in the bowl. Using a potato masher, mash up about half the beans in the bowl.

4. After mashing half the beans, give the mixture one more stir to make sure the beans are evenly mixed.

5. Drizzle the olive oil over the top.

6. Serve warm or cold with pita bread.

PREPARATION TIP: Try adding more color and spice to this recipe by finishing it off with a sprinkle of cayenne and fresh chopped parsley to the top.

STORAGE TIP: The leftovers can be stored in the fridge for up to 1 week and make a great lunch the next day.

PER SERVING: Calories: 199; Protein: 10g; Total Carbohydrates: 25g; Sugars: 4g; Fiber: 9g; Total Fat: 9g; Saturated Fat: 1g; Cholesterol: 0mg; Sodium: 395mg

Confetti Couscous

SERVES: 4 TO 6 | **PREP TIME:** 5 MINUTES | **COOK TIME:** 20 MINUTES

Couscous are little balls made of semolina or crushed durum wheat. Couscous is like a blank canvas that you can add flavor to. You can cook it plain and top it with a sauce or ragu, or you can cook it with different vegetables or meats. It is very easy to cook, similar to quinoa or rice.

3 tablespoons extra-virgin olive oil

1 large onion, chopped

» 2 carrots, chopped

» 1 cup fresh peas

» ½ cup golden raisins

1 teaspoon salt

» 2 cups vegetable broth

» 2 cups couscous

1. In a medium pot over medium heat, gently toss the olive oil, onions, carrots, peas, and raisins together and let cook for 5 minutes.

2. Add the salt and broth, and stir to combine. Bring to a boil, and let ingredients boil for 5 minutes.

3. Add the couscous. Stir, turn the heat to low, cover, and let cook for 10 minutes. Fluff with a fork and serve.

SUBSTITUTION TIP: You can substitute the peas or carrots for other vegetables of your choosing. Serve with fresh chopped parsley for extra flavor.

VARIATION TIP: Add in ½ teaspoon cinnamon along with the broth for a varied taste.

PER SERVING: Calories: 511; Protein: 14g; Total Carbohydrates: 92g; Sugars: 17g; Fiber: 7g; Total Fat: 12g; Saturated Fat: 2g; Cholesterol: 0mg; Sodium: 504mg

Lemon Orzo with Fresh Herbs

SERVES: 4 | **PREP TIME:** 10 MINUTES | **COOK TIME:** 10 MINUTES

This quick pasta dish inspires thoughts of spring and summer with fresh herbs and lemon. It's great for a fuss-free barbecue or potluck.

» 2 cups orzo

½ cup fresh parsley, finely chopped

½ cup fresh basil, finely chopped

» 2 tablespoons lemon zest

½ cup extra-virgin olive oil

⅓ cup lemon juice

1 teaspoon salt

½ teaspoon freshly ground black pepper

1. Bring a large pot of water to a boil. Add the orzo and cook for 7 minutes. Drain and rinse with cold water. Let the orzo sit in a strainer to completely drain and cool.

2. Once the orzo has cooled, put it in a large bowl and add the parsley, basil, and lemon zest.

3. In a small bowl, whisk together the olive oil, lemon juice, salt, and pepper. Add the dressing to the pasta and toss everything together. Serve at room temperature or chilled.

STORAGE TIP: You can make this ahead and store it in the fridge for up to 3 days. For an added protein kick, add a can of rinsed and drained garbanzo beans.

PER SERVING: Calories: 568; Protein: 11g; Total Carbohydrates: 65g; Sugars: 4g; Fiber: 4g; Total Fat: 29g; Saturated Fat: 4g; Cholesterol: 0mg; Sodium: 586mg

Orzo-Veggie Pilaf

SERVES: 6 | **PREP TIME:** 20 MINUTES | **COOK TIME:** 10 MINUTES

Orzo is a type of Italian pasta that's about twice the size of a grain of cooked rice. It is most commonly used in soups or to make a pasta salad.

» 2 cups orzo

» 1 pint (2 cups) cherry tomatoes, cut in half

» 1 cup Kalamata olives

½ cup fresh basil, finely chopped

½ cup extra-virgin olive oil

» ⅓ cup balsamic vinegar

1 teaspoon salt

½ teaspoon freshly ground black pepper

1. Bring a large pot of water to a boil. Add the orzo and cook for 7 minutes. Drain and rinse the orzo with cold water in a strainer.

2. Once the orzo has cooled, put it in a large bowl. Add the tomatoes, olives, and basil.

3. In a small bowl, whisk together the olive oil, vinegar, salt, and pepper. Add this dressing to the pasta and toss everything together. Serve at room temperature or chilled.

SUBSTITUTION TIP: This is a great basic recipe you can customize to suit your palate. You can add anything from sliced red onions to feta cheese. To add a hint of spice, add some freshly ground black pepper over the top.

PER SERVING: Calories: 476; Protein: 8g; Total Carbohydrates: 48g; Sugars: 3g; Fiber: 3g; Total Fat: 28g; Saturated Fat: 4g; Cholesterol: 0mg; Sodium: 851mg

Earthy Lentil and Rice Pilaf

SERVES: 6 | **PREP TIME:** 5 MINUTES | **COOK TIME:** 50 MINUTES

This recipe combines lentils and rice to bring you fiber and protein with fantastic flavor. The earthy flavor of the lentils and rice is elevated with the addition of a warming spice—cumin.

¼ cup extra-virgin olive oil

1 large onion, chopped

6 cups water

» 1 teaspoon ground cumin

1 teaspoon salt

» 2 cups brown lentils, picked over and rinsed

» 1 cup basmati rice

1. In a medium pot over medium heat, cook the olive oil and onions for 7 to 10 minutes until the edges are browned.

2. Turn the heat to high, add the water, cumin, and salt, and bring this mixture to a boil, boiling for about 3 minutes.

3. Add the lentils and turn the heat to medium-low. Cover the pot and cook for 20 minutes, stirring occasionally.

4. Stir in the rice and cover; cook for an additional 20 minutes.

5. Fluff the rice with a fork and serve warm.

VARIATION TIP: Serve with a garden salad, Greek yogurt, or tzatziki sauce.

PER SERVING: Calories: 397; Protein: 18g; Total Carbohydrates: 60g; Sugars: 4g; Fiber: 18g; Total Fat: 11g; Saturated Fat: 1g; Cholesterol: 0mg; Sodium: 396mg

Lentils and Bulgur with Caramelized Onions

SERVES: 6 | **PREP TIME:** 10 MINUTES | **COOK TIME:** 50 MINUTES

This makes for a great dish for dinner or meal-prepped lunches. The sweet caramelized onions add a ton of flavor and give a golden color to this recipe.

½ cup extra-virgin olive oil

4 large onions, chopped

2 teaspoons salt, divided

6 cups water

» 2 cups brown lentils, picked over and rinsed

1 teaspoon freshly ground black pepper

» 1 cup bulgur wheat #3

1. In a large pot over medium heat, cook and stir the olive oil, onions, and 1 teaspoon of salt for 12 to 15 minutes, until the onions are a medium brown/golden color.

2. Put half of the cooked onions in a bowl.

3. Add the water, remaining 1 teaspoon of salt, and lentils to the remaining onions. Stir. Cover and cook for 30 minutes.

4. Stir in the black pepper and bulgur, cover, and cook for 5 minutes. Fluff with a fork, cover, and let stand for another 5 minutes.

5. Spoon the lentils and bulgur onto a serving plate and top with the reserved onions. Serve warm.

STORAGE TIP: This recipe is great as a side dish or lunch. Make ahead and store in the fridge for up to 5 days.

PER SERVING: Calories: 479; Protein: 20g; Total Carbohydrates: 60g; Sugars: 7g; Fiber: 24g; Total Fat: 20g; Saturated Fat: 3g; Cholesterol: 0mg; Sodium: 789mg

Bulgur and Garbanzo Pilaf

SERVES: 4 TO 6 | **PREP TIME:** 5 MINUTES | **COOK TIME:** 20 MINUTES

This earthy, nutty pilaf makes a great main dish or side dish. The bulgur and beans are full of protein and complex carbohydrates.

3 tablespoons
extra-virgin olive oil

1 large onion, chopped

» 1 (16-ounce) can
garbanzo beans,
rinsed and drained

» 2 cups bulgur wheat #3,
rinsed and drained

1½ teaspoons salt

» ½ teaspoon cinnamon

4 cups water

1. In a large pot over medium heat, cook the olive oil and onion for 5 minutes.

2. Add the garbanzo beans and cook for another 5 minutes.

3. Add the bulgur, salt, cinnamon, and water and stir to combine. Cover the pot, turn the heat to low, and cook for 10 minutes.

4. When the cooking is done, fluff the pilaf with a fork. Cover and let sit for another 5 minutes.

VARIATION TIP: Garnish this dish with fresh chopped parsley, or pair it with a salad, tzatziki, or plain Greek yogurt.

PER SERVING: Calories: 462; Protein: 15g;
Total Carbohydrates: 76g; Sugars: 5g; Fiber: 19g;
Total Fat: 13g; Saturated Fat: 2g; Cholesterol: 0mg;
Sodium: 890mg

Spanish Rice

SERVES: 4 | **PREP TIME:** 10 MINUTES | **COOK TIME:** 20 MINUTES

Spanish rice is a great alternative to plain white rice. It's simple and quick to prepare.

2 tablespoons
extra-virgin olive oil

1 medium onion,
finely chopped

» 1 large tomato,
finely diced

» 2 tablespoons
tomato paste

» 1 teaspoon
smoked paprika

1 teaspoon salt

» 1½ cups basmati rice

3 cups water

1. In a medium pot over medium heat, cook the olive oil, onion, and tomato for 3 minutes.

2. Stir in the tomato paste, paprika, salt, and rice. Cook for 1 minute.

3. Add the water, cover the pot, and turn the heat to low. Cook for 12 minutes.

4. Gently toss the rice, cover, and cook for another 3 minutes.

VARIATION TIP: I like to add freshly chopped cilantro right at the end of cooking for the color and the peppery flavor from the cilantro leaves.

STORAGE TIP: This rice can be made ahead and stored in an airtight container in the fridge for up to 3 days.

PER SERVING: Calories: 328; Protein: 6g;
Total Carbohydrates: 60g; Sugars: 3g; Fiber: 2g;
Total Fat: 7g; Saturated Fat: 1g; Cholesterol: 0mg;
Sodium: 651mg

Garbanzo and Pita No-Bake Casserole

SERVES: 4 | **PREP TIME:** 10 MINUTES | **COOK TIME:** 10 MINUTES

This quick and easy casserole can be served any time of day. The tangy yogurt sauce complements the crunchy pita bread with the warm garbanzo beans.

» 4 cups Greek yogurt

3 cloves garlic, minced

1 teaspoon salt

» 2 (16-ounce) cans garbanzo beans, rinsed and drained

2 cups water

» 4 cups pita chips

» 5 tablespoons unsalted butter

1. In a large bowl, whisk together the yogurt, garlic, and salt. Set aside.

2. Put the garbanzo beans and water in a medium pot. Bring to a boil; let beans boil for about 5 minutes.

3. Pour the garbanzo beans and the liquid into a large casserole dish.

4. Top the beans with pita chips. Pour the yogurt sauce over the pita chip layer.

5. In a small saucepan, melt and brown the butter, about 3 minutes. Pour the brown butter over the yogurt sauce.

VARIATION TIP: Add ½ cup pine nuts to the butter as you're browning it for even more flavor and texture in this dish.

PER SERVING: Calories: 772; Protein: 39g; Total Carbohydrates: 73g; Sugars: 18g; Fiber: 13g; Total Fat: 36g; Saturated Fat: 15g; Cholesterol: 71mg; Sodium: 1,003mg

Creamy Garlic and Cheese Polenta

SERVES: 4 | **PREP TIME:** 5 MINUTES | **COOK TIME:** 30 MINUTES

Polenta is made of boiled cornmeal and has a texture similar to cream of wheat. There are several ways to make polenta, and this simple recipe is great for any day of the week.

» 4 tablespoons (½ stick) unsalted butter, divided

1 tablespoon garlic, finely chopped

4 cups water

1 teaspoon salt

» 1 cup polenta

» ¾ cup Parmesan cheese, divided

1. In a large pot over medium heat, cook 3 tablespoons of butter and the garlic for 2 minutes.

2. Add the water and salt, and bring to a boil. Add the polenta and immediately whisk until it starts to thicken, about 3 minutes. Turn the heat to low, cover, and cook for 25 minutes, whisking every 5 minutes.

3. Using a wooden spoon, stir in ½ cup of the Parmesan cheese.

4. To serve, pour the polenta into a large serving bowl. Sprinkle the top with the remaining 1 tablespoon butter and ¼ cup of remaining Parmesan cheese. Serve warm.

VARIATION TIP: You can add fresh herbs like basil or parsley when you serve. Or, you can add a protein such as grilled shrimp or chicken.

PER SERVING: Calories: 297; Protein: 9g; Total Carbohydrates: 28g; Sugars: 0g; Fiber: 2g; Total Fat: 16g; Saturated Fat: 10g; Cholesterol: 42mg; Sodium: 838mg

Mushroom Risotto

SERVES: 4 | **PREP TIME:** 10 MINUTES | **COOK TIME:** 30 MINUTES

Risotto is a traditional Italian rice dish somewhat similar to Spanish Paella. This dish is constantly stirred as it cooks very slowly to ensure that the rice does not clump or stick to the pot.

» 6 cups vegetable broth

3 tablespoons extra-virgin olive oil, divided

» 1 pound cremini mushrooms, cleaned and sliced

1 medium onion, finely chopped

2 cloves garlic, minced

» 1½ cups Arborio rice

1 teaspoon salt

» ½ cup freshly grated Parmesan cheese

½ teaspoon freshly ground black pepper

1. In a saucepan over medium heat, bring the broth to a low simmer.

2. In a large skillet over medium heat, cook 1 tablespoon olive oil and the sliced mushrooms for 5 to 7 minutes. Set cooked mushrooms aside.

3. In the same skillet over medium heat, add the 2 remaining tablespoons of olive oil, onion, and garlic. Cook for 3 minutes.

4. Add the rice, salt, and 1 cup of broth to the skillet. Stir the ingredients together and cook over low heat until most of the liquid is absorbed. Continue adding ½ cup of broth at a time, stirring until it is absorbed. Repeat until all of the broth is used up.

5. With the final addition of broth, add the cooked mushrooms, Parmesan cheese, and black pepper. Cook for 2 more minutes. Serve immediately.

VARIATION TIP: For a really creamy risotto, add ½ cup of heavy (whipping) cream with the cheese. For an added fresh flavor, top with fresh chopped parsley.

PER SERVING: Calories: 410; Protein: 11g; Total Carbohydrates: 65g; Sugars: 5g; Fiber: 3g; Total Fat: 12g; Saturated Fat: 3g; Cholesterol: 4mg; Sodium: 2,086mg

Vegan, Vegetarian, Dairy-free, Gluten-free

Hearty White Bean Stew

SERVES: 4 TO 6 | **PREP TIME:** 10 MINUTES | **COOK TIME:** 30 MINUTES

This hearty bean and vegetable stew is a great option for people who want protein and flavor without the meat.

3 tablespoons extra-virgin olive oil

1 large onion, chopped

» 1 (15-ounce) can diced tomatoes

» 2 (15-ounce) cans white cannellini beans

» 1 cup carrots, chopped

» 4 cups vegetable broth

1 teaspoon salt

» 1 (1-pound) bag baby spinach, washed

1. In a large pot over medium heat, cook the olive oil and onion for 5 minutes.

2. Add the tomatoes, beans, carrots, broth, and salt. Stir and cook for 20 minutes.

3. Add the spinach, a handful at a time, and cook for 5 minutes, until the spinach has wilted.

4. Serve warm.

VARIATION TIP: You can add additional vegetables to the stew, like celery or green peas, to add more color and flavor.

PER SERVING: Calories: 356; Protein: 15g; Total Carbohydrates: 47g; Sugars: 10g; Fiber: 16g; Total Fat: 12g; Saturated Fat: 2g; Cholesterol: 0mg; Sodium: 1,832mg

White Pizza with Prosciutto and Arugula, Page 73

CHAPTER 6

Pastas, Pizzas, and Breads

Where would the world be without pasta, pizza, and bread? I would hate to know. This chapter takes you through the Mediterranean and explores how you can take a simple dough and turn it into a flavorful piece of bread with a crunchy outside and cloud-like inside. It also shows how you can make a simple pasta dish flavorful by adding some robust ingredients. These recipes are simple and fast, but taste like they came out of a restaurant kitchen.

Herb-Topped Focaccia

SERVES: 10 | **PREP TIME:** 2 HOURS | **COOK TIME:** 20 MINUTES

Focaccia is an Italian bread that is about an inch thick and seasoned with herbs and olive oil. It's usually a square shape and has a crunchy crust. This bread can be eaten any time of day and used to dip in a sauce or to make a sandwich.

» 1 tablespoon dried rosemary or 3 tablespoons minced fresh rosemary

1 tablespoon dried thyme or 3 tablespoons minced fresh thyme leaves

½ cup extra-virgin olive oil

» 1 teaspoon sugar

1 cup warm water

» 1 (¼-ounce) packet active dry yeast

» 2½ cups flour, divided

1 teaspoon salt

1. In a small bowl, combine the rosemary and thyme with the olive oil.

2. In a large bowl, whisk together the sugar, water, and yeast. Let stand for 5 minutes.

3. Add 1 cup of flour, half of the olive oil mixture, and the salt to the mixture in the large bowl. Stir to combine.

4. Add the remaining 1½ cups flour to the large bowl. Using your hands, combine dough until it starts to pull away from the sides of the bowl.

5. Put the dough on a floured board or countertop and knead 10 to 12 times. Place the dough in a well-oiled bowl and cover with plastic wrap. Put it in a warm, dry space for 1 hour.

6. Oil a 9-by-13-inch baking pan. Turn the dough onto the baking pan, and using your hands gently push the dough out to fit the pan.

7. Using your fingers, make dimples into the dough. Evenly pour the remaining half of the olive oil mixture over the dough. Let the dough rise for another 30 minutes.

8. Preheat the oven to 450°F. Place the dough into the oven and let cook for 18 to 20 minutes, until you see it turn a golden brown.

SUBSTITUTION TIP: You can use any herbs you like for this dough. For example, you can use oregano and basil if you prefer. You can also add things like chopped olives and garlic.

PER SERVING: Calories: 199; Protein: 3g; Total Carbohydrates: 23g; Sugars: 0g; Fiber: 1g; Total Fat: 11g; Saturated Fat: 2g; Cholesterol: 0mg; Sodium: 233mg

Vegetarian

Caramelized Onion Flatbread with Arugula

SERVES: 4 | **PREP TIME:** 10 MINUTES | **COOK TIME:** 25 MINUTES

Onions are so versatile because they are so pungent in flavor when raw, and yet so sweet when you cook them down. This recipe may seem fancy, but it is very easy to make and will impress your guests.

4 tablespoons extra-virgin olive oil, divided

2 large onions, sliced into ¼-inch-thick slices

1 teaspoon salt, divided

» 1 sheet puff pastry

» 1 (5-ounce) package goat cheese

» 8 ounces arugula

½ teaspoon freshly ground black pepper

1. Preheat the oven to 400°F.

2. In a large skillet over medium heat, cook 3 tablespoons olive oil, the onions, and ½ teaspoon of salt, stirring, for 10 to 12 minutes, until the onions are translucent and golden brown.

3. To assemble, line a baking sheet with parchment paper. Lay the puff pastry flat on the parchment paper. Prick the middle of the puff pastry all over with a fork, leaving a ½-inch border.

4. Evenly distribute the onions on the pastry, leaving the border.

5. Crumble the goat cheese over the onions. Put the pastry in the oven to bake for 10 to 12 minutes, or until you see the border become golden brown.

6. Remove the pastry from the oven, set aside. In a medium bowl, add the arugula, remaining 1 tablespoon of olive oil, remaining ½ teaspoon of salt, and ½ teaspoon black pepper; toss to evenly dress the arugula.

7. Cut the pastry into even squares. Top the pastry with dressed arugula and serve.

SUBSTITUTION TIP: If you don't like goat cheese, you can use ricotta cheese for a milder flavor.

PER SERVING: Calories: 501; Protein: 12g; Total Carbohydrates: 29g; Sugars: 5g; Fiber: 4g; Total Fat: 40g; Saturated Fat: 10g; Cholesterol: 44mg; Sodium: 878mg

Quick Shrimp Fettuccine

SERVES: 4 TO 6 | **PREP TIME:** 10 MINUTES | **COOK TIME:** 10 MINUTES

This recipe makes a great weeknight dish because shrimp is a fast-cooking protein. The garlic and lemon flavors complement the shrimp and make a zesty sauce for the pasta.

» 8 ounces fettuccine pasta

¼ cup extra-virgin olive oil

3 tablespoons garlic, minced

» 1 pound large shrimp (21-25), peeled and deveined

⅓ cup lemon juice

» 1 tablespoon lemon zest

½ teaspoon salt

½ teaspoon freshly ground black pepper

1. Bring a large pot of salted water to a boil. Add the fettuccine and cook for 8 minutes.

2. In a large saucepan over medium heat, cook the olive oil and garlic for 1 minute.

3. Add the shrimp to the saucepan and cook for 3 minutes on each side. Remove the shrimp from the pan and set aside.

4. Add the lemon juice and lemon zest to the saucepan, along with the salt and pepper.

5. Reserve ½ cup of the pasta water and drain the pasta.

6. Add the pasta water to the saucepan with the lemon juice and zest and stir everything together. Add the pasta and toss together to evenly coat the pasta. Transfer the pasta to a serving dish and top with the cooked shrimp. Serve warm.

VARIATION TIP: You can add 1 cup of heavy (whipping) cream to the sauce in the pan and let it simmer for 2 minutes. Top if off with 2 tablespoons of freshly chopped basil for a creamy texture and more flavor.

PER SERVING: Calories: 615; Protein: 33g; Total Carbohydrates: 89g; Sugars: 3g; Fiber: 4g; Total Fat: 17g; Saturated Fat: 2g; Cholesterol: 145mg; Sodium: 407mg

Simple Pesto Pasta

SERVES: 4 TO 6 | **PREP TIME:** 10 MINUTES | **COOK TIME:** 10 MINUTES

Pesto is one of the easiest sauces or spreads that you can make. All you have to do is throw everything into a food processor and chop it up. The robust flavor of basil and garlic make pesto a fantastic sauce for pasta and a flavorful topping for chicken or fish. It can even be used as a sandwich spread.

» 1 pound spaghetti

4 cups fresh basil leaves, stems removed

3 cloves garlic

1 teaspoon salt

½ teaspoon freshly ground black pepper

¼ cup lemon juice

» ½ cup pine nuts, toasted

» ½ cup grated Parmesan cheese

1 cup extra-virgin olive oil

1. Bring a large pot of salted water to a boil. Add the spaghetti to the pot and cook for 8 minutes.

2. Put basil, garlic, salt, pepper, lemon juice, pine nuts, and Parmesan cheese in a food processor bowl with chopping blade and purée.

3. While the processor is running, slowly drizzle the olive oil through the top opening. Process until all the olive oil has been added.

4. Reserve ½ cup of the pasta water. Drain the pasta and put it into a bowl. Immediately add the pesto and pasta water to the pasta and toss everything together. Serve warm.

VARIATION TIP: Serve with grilled fish or chicken and top with freshly grated Parmesan cheese and freshly ground black pepper.

PER SERVING: Calories: 1,067; Protein: 23g; Total Carbohydrates: 91g; Sugars: 3g; Fiber: 6g; Total Fat: 72g; Saturated Fat: 11g; Cholesterol: 10mg; Sodium: 817mg

Za'atar Pizza

SERVES: 4 TO 6 | **PREP TIME:** 10 MINUTES | **COOK TIME:** 15 MINUTES

Za'atar is a Middle Eastern flavoring mix made of dried thyme, ground sumac, and toasted sesame seeds. It's great for seasoning breads or chicken. This is a quick way to make a pizza with a lot of flavor and no cheese.

» 1 sheet puff pastry

¼ cup extra-virgin olive oil

» ⅓ cup za'atar seasoning

1. Preheat the oven to 350°F.

2. Put the puff pastry on a parchment-lined baking sheet. Cut the pastry into desired slices.

3. Brush the pastry with olive oil. Sprinkle with the za'atar.

4. Put the pastry in the oven and bake for 10 to 12 minutes or until edges are lightly browned and puffed up. Serve warm or at room temperature.

VARIATION TIP: Serve with Greek yogurt or tzatziki sauce.

PER SERVING: Calories: 374; Protein: 3g; Total Carbohydrates: 20g; Sugars: 1g; Fiber: 1g; Total Fat: 30g; Saturated Fat: 6g; Cholesterol: 0mg; Sodium: 166mg

White Pizza with Prosciutto and Arugula

SERVES: 4 | **PREP TIME:** 10 MINUTES | **COOK TIME:** 15 MINUTES

White pizza is a good alternative for those that don't like the traditional red sauce. The cured prosciutto and lemony basil add some salt and sweetness to this dish.

» 1 pound prepared pizza dough

» ½ cup ricotta cheese

1 tablespoon garlic, minced

» 1 cup grated mozzarella cheese

» 3 ounces prosciutto, thinly sliced

½ cup fresh arugula

½ teaspoon freshly ground black pepper

1. Preheat the oven to 450°F. Roll out the pizza dough on a floured surface.

2. Put the pizza dough on a parchment-lined baking sheet or pizza sheet. Put the dough in the oven and bake for 8 minutes.

3. In a small bowl, mix together the ricotta, garlic, and mozzarella.

4. Remove the pizza dough from the oven and spread the cheese mixture over the top. Bake for another 5 to 6 minutes.

5. Top the pizza with prosciutto, arugula, and pepper; serve warm.

SUBSTITUTION TIP: If you don't like arugula, you can top the pizza with basil dressed with some olive oil, salt, and pepper.

PER SERVING: Calories: 435; Protein: 20g; Total Carbohydrates: 51g; Sugars: 0g; Fiber: 4g; Total Fat: 17g; Saturated Fat: 8g; Cholesterol: 53mg; Sodium: 1,630mg

Flat Meat Pies

SERVES: 4 | **PREP TIME:** 20 MINUTES | **COOK TIME:** 15 MINUTES

Meat pies look like mini pizzas but without the cheese. This recipe is great because you can make the meat pies, freeze them, and warm them up when you need a quick dinner.

» ½ pound ground beef

1 small onion,
finely chopped

» 1 medium tomato, finely
diced and strained

½ teaspoon salt

½ teaspoon freshly
ground black pepper

» 2 sheets puff pastry

1. Preheat the oven to 400°F.

2. In a medium bowl, combine the beef, onion, tomato, salt, and pepper. Set aside.

3. Line 2 baking sheets with parchment paper. Cut the puff pastry dough into 4-inch squares and lay them flat on the baking sheets.

4. Scoop about 2 tablespoons of beef mixture onto each piece of dough. Spread the meat on the dough, leaving a ½-inch edge on each side.

5. Put the meat pies in the oven and bake for 12 to 15 minutes until edges are golden brown.

STORAGE TIP: After you bake the pies, store them in a container or plastic zip-top bag in the freezer for up to 1 month. To heat them up, just preheat the oven to 350°F and bake for 7 minutes.

PER SERVING: Calories: 577; Protein: 18g; Total Carbohydrates: 41g; Sugars: 2g; Fiber: 2g; Total Fat: 38g; Saturated Fat: 10g; Cholesterol: 35mg; Sodium: 541mg

Freezer Friendly

Meaty Baked Penne

SERVES: 8 | **PREP TIME:** 10 MINUTES | **COOK TIME:** 40 MINUTES

This baked pasta is great for a weekday dinner because it's easy to make and full of flavor. You won't need any other side dishes when you make this; you'll get your veggies, protein, and carbs all in this recipe.

» 1 pound penne pasta

» 1 pound ground beef

1 teaspoon salt

» 1 (25-ounce) jar marinara sauce

» 1 (1-pound) bag baby spinach, washed

» 3 cups shredded mozzarella cheese, divided

1. Bring a large pot of salted water to a boil, add the penne, and cook for 7 minutes. Reserve 2 cups of the pasta water and drain the pasta.

2. Preheat the oven to 350°F.

3. In a large saucepan over medium heat, cook the ground beef and salt. Brown the ground beef for about 5 minutes.

4. Stir in marinara sauce, and 2 cups of pasta water. Let simmer for 5 minutes.

5. Add a handful of spinach at a time into the sauce, and cook for another 3 minutes.

6. To assemble, in a 9-by-13-inch baking dish, add the pasta and pour the pasta sauce over it. Stir in 1½ cups of the mozzarella cheese. Cover the dish with foil and bake for 20 minutes.

7. After 20 minutes, remove the foil, top with the rest of the mozzarella, and bake for another 10 minutes. Serve warm.

VARIATION TIP: For more veggies, you can add sautéed mushrooms or cooked chopped onions.

PER SERVING: Calories: 497; Protein: 31g; Total Carbohydrates: 54g; Sugars: 7g; Fiber: 5g; Total Fat: 18g; Saturated Fat: 8g; Cholesterol: 68mg; Sodium: 1,083mg

Cheesy Spaghetti with Pine Nuts

SERVES: 4 TO 6 | **PREP TIME:** 10 MINUTES | **COOK TIME:** 10 MINUTES

This is another version of a popular Italian dish called *Cacio e pepe*, which translates as cheese and pepper. I like to add toasted pine nuts to this recipe because they add so much more flavor and texture.

» 8 ounces spaghetti

» 4 tablespoons (½ stick) unsalted butter

1 teaspoon freshly ground black pepper

» ½ cup pine nuts

» 1 cup fresh grated Parmesan cheese, divided

1. Bring a large pot of salted water to a boil. Add the pasta and cook for 8 minutes.

2. In a large saucepan over medium heat, combine the butter, black pepper, and pine nuts. Cook for 2 to 3 minutes or until the pine nuts are lightly toasted.

3. Reserve ½ cup of the pasta water. Drain the pasta and put it into the pan with the pine nuts.

4. Add ¾ cup of Parmesan cheese and the reserved pasta water to the pasta and toss everything together to evenly coat the pasta.

5. To serve, put the pasta in a serving dish and top with the remaining ¼ cup of Parmesan cheese.

SUBSTITUTION TIP: You can also replace ⅓ cup of Parmesan cheese with pecorino cheese for added flavor.

PER SERVING: Calories: 542; Protein: 20g; Total Carbohydrates: 46g; Sugars: 2g; Fiber: 2g; Total Fat: 32g; Saturated Fat: 13g; Cholesterol: 51mg; Sodium: 552mg

Creamy Garlic-Parmesan Chicken Pasta

SERVES: 4 | **PREP TIME:** 5 MINUTES | **COOK TIME:** 25 MINUTES

Chicken is great protein for pasta because it pairs well with any sauce. This simple recipe is flavored with garlic and Parmesan cheese.

» 2 boneless, skinless chicken breasts

3 tablespoons extra-virgin olive oil

1½ teaspoons salt

1 large onion, thinly sliced

3 tablespoons garlic, minced

» 1 pound fettuccine pasta

» 1 cup heavy (whipping) cream

» ¾ cup freshly grated Parmesan cheese, divided

½ teaspoon freshly ground black pepper

1. Bring a large pot of salted water to a simmer.

2. Cut the chicken into thin strips.

3. In a large skillet over medium heat, cook the olive oil and chicken for 3 minutes.

4. Next add the salt, onion, and garlic to the pan with the chicken. Cook for 7 minutes.

5. Bring the pot of salted water to a boil and add the pasta, then let it cook for 7 minutes.

6. While the pasta is cooking, add the cream, ½ cup of Parmesan cheese, and black pepper to the chicken; simmer for 3 minutes.

7. Reserve ½ cup of the pasta water. Drain the pasta and add it to the chicken cream sauce.

8. Add the reserved pasta water to the pasta and toss together. Let simmer for 2 minutes. Top with the remaining ¼ cup Parmesan cheese and serve warm.

VARIATION TIP: Frozen or fresh green peas and sautéed mushrooms are also a great addition to this recipe. Adding fresh herbs like parsley or basil will further deepen the flavor.

PER SERVING: Calories: 879; Protein: 35g; Total Carbohydrates: 90g; Sugars: 7g; Fiber: 5g; Total Fat: 42g; Saturated Fat: 19g; Cholesterol: 129mg; Sodium: 1,336mg

SMOKY HERB LAMB CHOPS AND
LEMON-ROSEMARY DRESSING, PAGE 92

CHAPTER 7

Poultry and Meat

The Mediterranean countryside is perfect for raising livestock such as cattle, sheep, and chickens. Most of the countryside is lush with green fields that are optimal for these animals to graze and grow. In this chapter, we explore simple, easy-to-find ingredients and turn them into something that tastes like it came from Grandma's kitchen. Mediterranean cooking frequently takes what commonly grows on the land and pairs it with different meats or vegetables, resulting in a recipe that becomes a family favorite.

Za'atar Chicken

SERVES: 4 TO 6 | **PREP TIME:** 5 MINUTES | **COOK TIME:** 40 MINUTES

Za'atar is a very common spice mix used in the Middle East region of the Mediterranean. It has a lot of flavor from the dried thyme and sumac. It is most commonly used in baking and salads, but is also great for adding a warm, earthy flavor to chicken or fish.

» ⅓ cup plus 1 tablespoon za'atar spice

2 tablespoons garlic, minced

⅓ cup lemon juice

⅓ cup extra-virgin olive oil

1 teaspoon salt

» 8 pieces chicken thighs and drumsticks, skin on

1. Preheat the oven to 400°F.

2. In a small bowl, combine the ⅓ cup za'atar spice with the garlic, lemon juice, olive oil, and salt.

3. Place the chicken in a baking dish, and pat dry with a paper towel.

4. Pour the za'atar mixture over the chicken, making sure the pieces are completely and evenly coated.

5. Put the chicken in the oven and cook for 40 minutes.

6. Once the chicken is done cooking, sprinkle it with the remaining tablespoon of za'atar spice. Serve with potatoes, rice, or salad.

SUBSTITUTION TIP: If you do not like using chicken thighs or drumsticks, you can use chicken breasts or boneless chicken with the skin. The skin helps prevent the chicken from drying out in the oven.

PER SERVING: Calories: 505; Protein: 31g; Total Carbohydrates: 4g; Sugars: 1g; Fiber: 0g; Total Fat: 39g; Saturated Fat: 8g; Cholesterol: 138mg; Sodium: 775mg

Chicken Shawarma

SERVES: 4 TO 6 | **PREP TIME:** 15 MINUTES | **COOK TIME:** 15 MINUTES

Shawarma is a classic method to cook spiced lamb or veal. It is traditionally cooked on a vertical rotisserie. This recipe allows you to make it at home with the same flavors but less equipment. Chicken shawarma has a mild spice flavor combined with citrus and garlic.

» 2 pounds boneless and skinless chicken

½ cup lemon juice

½ cup extra-virgin olive oil

3 tablespoons minced garlic

1½ teaspoons salt

½ teaspoon freshly ground black pepper

» ½ teaspoon ground cardamom

» ½ teaspoon cinnamon

Hummus and pita bread, for serving (optional)

1. Cut the chicken into ¼-inch strips and put them into a large bowl.

2. In a separate bowl, whisk together the lemon juice, olive oil, garlic, salt, pepper, cardamom, and cinnamon.

3. Pour the dressing over the chicken and stir to coat all of the chicken.

4. Let the chicken sit for about 10 minutes.

5. Heat a large pan over medium-high heat and cook the chicken pieces for 12 minutes, using tongs to turn the chicken over every few minutes.

6. Serve with hummus and pita bread, if desired.

PREPARATION TIP: You can marinate the chicken in the dressing for up to 2 days in the fridge.

PER SERVING: Calories: 477; Protein: 47g; Total Carbohydrates: 5g; Sugars: 1g; Fiber: 1g; Total Fat: 32g; Saturated Fat: 5g; Cholesterol: 130mg; Sodium: 1,234mg

Italian Herb Grilled Chicken

SERVES: 4 | **PREP TIME:** 20 MINUTES | **COOK TIME:** 10 MINUTES

Grilled chicken can often seem boring because it easily can be too bland or overcooked. This recipe is a great way of infusing the chicken with spices and herbs and grilling it to perfection.

½ cup lemon juice

½ cup extra-virgin olive oil

3 tablespoons garlic, minced

» 2 teaspoons dried oregano

» 1 teaspoon red pepper flakes

1 teaspoon salt

» 2 pounds boneless and skinless chicken breasts

1. In a large bowl, mix together the lemon juice, olive oil, garlic, oregano, red pepper flakes, and salt.

2. Fillet the chicken breast in half horizontally to get 2 thin pieces, repeating with all of the breasts.

3. Put the chicken in the bowl with the marinade and let sit for at least 10 minutes before cooking.

4. Preheat a grill, grill pan, or lightly oiled skillet to high heat. Once hot, cook the chicken for 4 minutes on each side. Serve warm.

PREPARATION TIP: You can marinate the chicken in the fridge for up to a day in advance. This will also enhance the flavor.

PER SERVING: Calories: 479; Protein: 47g; Total Carbohydrates: 5g; Sugars: 1g; Fiber: 1g; Total Fat: 32g; Saturated Fat: 5g; Cholesterol: 130mg; Sodium: 943mg

Garlic Chicken (Shish Tawook)

SERVES: 4 TO 6 | **PREP TIME:** 15 MINUTES | **COOK TIME:** 15 MINUTES

Shish Tawook is a traditional marinated chicken dish. This recipe gives grilled chicken a boost of flavor. But if you don't want to grill, you can still enjoy this recipe by cooking it in a pan.

2 tablespoons garlic, minced

» 2 tablespoons tomato paste

» 1 teaspoon smoked paprika

½ cup lemon juice

½ cup extra-virgin olive oil

1½ teaspoons salt

½ teaspoon freshly ground black pepper

» 2 pounds boneless and skinless chicken (breasts or thighs)

Rice, tzatziki, or hummus, for serving (optional)

1. In a large bowl, add the garlic, tomato paste, paprika, lemon juice, olive oil, salt, and pepper and whisk to combine.

2. Cut the chicken into ½-inch cubes and put them into the bowl; toss to coat with the marinade. Set aside for at least 10 minutes.

3. To grill, preheat the grill on high. Thread the chicken onto skewers and cook for 3 minutes per side, for a total of 9 minutes.

4. To cook in a pan, preheat the pan on high heat, add the chicken, and cook for 9 minutes, turning over the chicken using tongs.

5. Serve the chicken with rice, tzatziki, or hummus, if desired.

PREPARATION TIP: This meal freezes well. Prepare the chicken through step two, divide the marinated chicken into meal-size portions, and store in freezer safe bags or containers. To cook, take the chicken out of the freezer, defrost, and continue with the directions.

PER SERVING: Calories: 482; Protein: 47g; Total Carbohydrates: 6g; Sugars: 2g; Fiber: 1g; Total Fat: 32g; Saturated Fat: 5g; Cholesterol: 130mg; Sodium: 1,298mg

Braised Chicken and Mushrooms

SERVES: 4 | **PREP TIME:** 20 MINUTES | **COOK TIME:** 1 HOUR 30 MINUTES

This is a braised chicken recipe with lots of garlic and mushrooms to add flavor to the chicken. The slow cooking turns the garlic into sweet nuggets, while the chicken becomes juicy and tender.

3 tablespoons extra-virgin olive oil

» 8 pieces chicken, thighs and drumsticks

1½ cups garlic cloves, peeled

1 large onion, chopped

» 1 pound cremini mushrooms, cleaned and cut in half

1 teaspoon salt

» 4 cups chicken broth

Rice or noodles, for serving (optional)

1. In a large pot or Dutch oven over medium heat, heat the olive oil and add chicken, browning on all sides, for about 8 minutes. Remove the chicken and place onto a dish; set aside.

2. Add the garlic, onion, mushrooms, and salt to the pot. Stir and cook for 8 minutes.

3. Add the broth to the pot and stir everything together. Add the chicken back into the pot, cover, and turn the heat to medium-low. Let simmer for 1 hour.

4. Uncover the pot and let simmer for another 10 minutes.

5. Serve with rice or noodles, if desired.

VARIATION TIP: Finish off the recipe with fresh chopped parsley for color and flavor.

PER SERVING: Calories: 521; Protein: 38g; Total Carbohydrates: 24g; Sugars: 3g; Fiber: 3g; Total Fat: 31g; Saturated Fat: 7g; Cholesterol: 138mg; Sodium: 742mg

Garlic-Lemon Chicken and Potatoes

SERVES: 4 TO 6 | **PREP TIME:** 10 MINUTES | **COOK TIME:** 45 MINUTES

The chicken and potatoes take on a citrus flavor from baking in the garlicky lemon sauce. This is a hearty recipe that is sure to make you and your guests happy on any night of the week.

1 cup garlic, minced

1½ cups lemon juice

1 cup plus 2 tablespoons extra-virgin olive oil, divided

1½ teaspoons salt, divided

1 teaspoon freshly ground black pepper

» 1 whole chicken, cut into 8 pieces

» 1 pound fingerling or red potatoes

1. Preheat the oven to 400°F.

2. In a large bowl, whisk together the garlic, lemon juice, 1 cup of olive oil, 1 teaspoon of salt, and pepper.

3. Put the chicken in a large baking dish and pour half of the lemon sauce over the chicken. Cover the baking dish with foil, and cook for 20 minutes.

4. Cut the potatoes in half, and toss to coat with 2 tablespoons olive oil and 1 teaspoon of salt. Put them on a baking sheet and bake for 20 minutes in the same oven as the chicken.

5. Take both the chicken and potatoes out of the oven. Using a spatula, transfer the potatoes to the baking dish with the chicken. Pour the remaining sauce over the potatoes and chicken. Bake for another 25 minutes.

6. Transfer the chicken and potatoes to a serving dish and spoon the garlic-lemon sauce from the pan on top.

VARIATION TIP: Instead of using bone-in chicken, you can use boneless and skinless chicken thighs and prepare it the same way.

PER SERVING: Calories: 959; Protein: 33g; Total Carbohydrates: 37g; Sugars: 4g; Fiber: 4g; Total Fat: 78g; Saturated Fat: 13g; Cholesterol: 80mg; Sodium: 1,005mg

Whole-Roasted Spanish Chicken

SERVES: 4 | **PREP TIME:** 1 HOUR | **COOK TIME:** 55 MINUTES

Roasted chicken is great for a Sunday meal with family and friends. It is easy to both prepare and cook, allowing you to focus on the sides. The smoky paprika and citrusy lemon zest gives the chicken—especially the crispy skin—a tangy flavor.

» 4 tablespoons (½ stick) unsalted butter, softened

» 2 tablespoons lemon zest

» 2 tablespoons smoked paprika

2 tablespoons garlic, minced

1½ teaspoons salt

1 teaspoon freshly ground black pepper

» 1 5-pound whole chicken, skin on

1. In a small bowl, combine the butter with the lemon zest, paprika, garlic, salt, and pepper.

2. Pat the chicken dry using a paper towel. Using your hands, rub the seasoned butter all over the chicken. Refrigerate the chicken for 30 minutes.

3. Preheat the oven to 425°F. Take the chicken out of the fridge and let it sit out for 20 minutes.

4. Put the chicken in a baking dish in the oven and let it cook for 20 minutes. Turn the temperature down to 350°F and let the chicken cook for another 35 minutes.

5. Take the chicken out of the oven and let it stand for 10 minutes before serving.

SUBSTITUTION TIP: If you can't have butter, you can replace it with ⅓ cup extra-virgin olive oil.

PER SERVING: Calories: 1,322; Protein: 106g; Total Carbohydrates: 4g; Sugars: 1g; Fiber: 2g; Total Fat: 97g; Saturated Fat: 30g; Cholesterol: 531mg; Sodium: 1,276mg

Mediterranean Pork Chops

SERVES: 4 | **PREP TIME:** 20 MINUTES | **COOK TIME:** 10 MINUTES

Pork is a great canvas for flavor. There are so many herbs or spices that you can use with pork. But it can also be tricky to cook because it can easily dry out. This simple recipe can be made any night of the week; it has just enough flavor from the herbs and spices to wake up your taste buds.

¼ cup extra-virgin olive oil

» 1 teaspoon smoked paprika

2 tablespoons fresh thyme leaves

1 teaspoon salt

» 4 pork loin chops, ½-inch-thick

1. In a small bowl, mix together the olive oil, paprika, thyme, and salt.

2. Put the pork chops in a plastic zip-top bag or a bowl and coat them with the spice mix. Let them marinate for 15 minutes.

3. Preheat a grill, grill pan, or lightly oiled skillet to high heat. Cook the pork chops for 4 minutes on each side. Serve with a Greek salad.

PREPARATION TIP: This is also a great make-ahead recipe. Marinate the pork chops in the morning, keep them covered in the marinade in the refrigerator, and cook the chops for dinner. This will also bring out the flavor from the paprika and thyme.

PER SERVING: Calories: 282; Protein: 21g; Total Carbohydrates: 1g; Sugars: 0g; Fiber: 0g; Total Fat: 23g; Saturated Fat: 5g; Cholesterol: 55mg; Sodium: 832mg

Pork Souvlaki

SERVES: 4 | **PREP TIME:** 1 HOUR 15 MINUTES | **COOK TIME:** 10 MINUTES

Souvlaki kebabs are a traditional and flavorful Greek dish. Souvlaki can be made with lamb, beef, chicken, or pork. These souvlaki are infused with flavor from the tangy lemon and herbs.

» 1 (1½-pound) pork loin

2 tablespoons garlic, minced

⅓ cup extra-virgin olive oil

⅓ cup lemon juice

» 1 tablespoon dried oregano

1 teaspoon salt

Pita bread and tzatziki, for serving (optional)

1. Cut the pork into 1-inch cubes and put them into a bowl or plastic zip-top bag.

2. In a large bowl, mix together the garlic, olive oil, lemon juice, oregano, and salt.

3. Pour the marinade over the pork and let it marinate for at least 1 hour.

4. Preheat a grill, grill pan, or lightly oiled skillet to high heat. Using wood or metal skewers, thread the pork onto the skewers.

5. Cook the skewers for 3 minutes on each side, for 12 minutes in total.

6. Serve with pita bread and tzatziki sauce, if desired.

PREPARATION TIP: Whenever using wood skewers, make sure to soak them in water for 5 minutes before using; that way the skewers will not burn.

PER SERVING: Calories: 416; Protein: 32g; Total Carbohydrates: 5g; Sugars: 1g; Fiber: 1g; Total Fat: 30g; Saturated Fat: 7g; Cholesterol: 82mg; Sodium: 1,184mg

Bold Chorizo Paella

SERVES: 4 | **PREP TIME:** 5 MINUTES | **COOK TIME:** 30 MINUTES

Paella is a traditional Spanish dish with many variations, but the main ingredient is the rice with saffron and paprika. These spices add a bold flavor and beautiful rust color.

3 tablespoons extra-virgin olive oil

1 large onion, chopped

2 cloves garlic, minced

» 2 tablespoons tomato paste

» 1 teaspoon paprika

» 1 teaspoon saffron threads

» 1 pound Spanish chorizo sausage

» 2 cups Bomba or Arborio rice

1½ teaspoons salt

5 cups water

1. In a large, deep skillet over medium heat, cook the olive oil and onion for 3 to 5 minutes. Add garlic and cook for another minute.

2. Stir in the tomato paste, paprika, and saffron. Stir in the chorizo and rice, and cook for 3 minutes.

3. Add the salt and water. Stir to combine, turn heat to low, and let simmer for 10 minutes. Give the rice a gentle stir and cook for another 12 to 15 minutes.

4. Serve warm.

VARIATION TIP: You can add vegetables such as peas, peppers, or carrots just after you sauté the onions. If you want to add shrimp, put them in the rice after the first 10 minutes of cooking. Sprinkle with fresh parsley.

PER SERVING: Calories: 747; Protein: 23g; Total Carbohydrates: 76g; Sugars: 2g; Fiber: 2g; Total Fat: 39g; Saturated Fat: 12g; Cholesterol: 80mg; Sodium: 1,593mg

Braised Lamb Shanks

SERVES: 4 TO 6 | **PREP TIME:** 10 MINUTES | **COOK TIME:** 2 HOURS

Braised lamb shanks are cooked low and slow so that you get tender and flavorful meat. This may not be a weeknight recipe if you are looking for something quick, but definitely something you can do in a slow cooker and cook all day while you are at work.

3 tablespoons extra-virgin olive oil

» 6 lamb shanks

1 large onion, chopped

» 3 carrots, chopped

» 1 (15-ounce) can diced tomatoes

6 cups water

» 3 bay leaves

1 teaspoon salt

1. Place a large pot with a lid or Dutch oven over high heat and add the olive oil and lamb shanks. Brown on each side, about 8 minutes total.

2. Put the shanks onto a plate and add the onion and carrots to the same pot; cook for 5 minutes.

3. Add the tomatoes, water, bay leaves, and salt. Stir to combine. Add the lamb shanks back to the pot and bring to a simmer.

4. Turn the heat down to low and cover the pot. Let the shanks cook for 1 hour and 30 minutes. Remove the cover and let cook for another 20 minutes.

5. Remove the bay leaves from the pot and spoon the lamb shanks and sauce onto a serving dish. Serve warm with rice or couscous.

PREPARATION TIP: If you want to reduce the cooking time, use a pressure cooker and cut the cook time to 45 minutes. Or, you can follow steps 1 through 3 in a pot, then transfer everything to a slow cooker and cook on low for 4 to 6 hours.

PER SERVING: Calories: 538; Protein: 45g; Total Carbohydrates: 11g; Sugars: 6g; Fiber: 3g; Total Fat: 34g; Saturated Fat: 12g; Cholesterol: 141mg; Sodium: 920mg

Greek Lamb Burgers

SERVES: 4 | **PREP TIME:** 10 MINUTES | **COOK TIME:** 10 MINUTES

This is definitely different than your regular beef burger. This burger has a surprise of feta cheese in the center that adds a burst of flavor to the lamb. You can easily turn this into a gourmet burger with fancy toppings like sautéed mushrooms or Dijon mustard.

» 1 pound ground lamb

½ teaspoon salt

½ teaspoon freshly ground black pepper

» 4 tablespoons feta cheese, crumbled

Buns, toppings, and tzatziki, for serving (optional)

1. Preheat a grill, grill pan, or lightly oiled skillet to high heat.

2. In a large bowl, using your hands, combine the lamb with the salt and pepper.

3. Divide the meat into 4 portions. Divide each portion in half to make a top and a bottom. Flatten each half into a 3-inch circle. Make a dent in the center of one of the halves and place 1 tablespoon of the feta cheese in the center. Place the second half of the patty on top of the feta cheese and press down to close the 2 halves together, making it resemble a round burger.

4. Cook the stuffed patty for 3 minutes on each side, for medium-well. Serve on a bun with your favorite toppings and tzatziki sauce, if desired.

VARIATION TIP: You can add a teaspoon of fresh thyme or chopped rosemary to the lamb for even more great taste.

PER SERVING: Calories: 345; Protein: 20g; Total Carbohydrates: 1g; Sugars: 0g; Fiber: 0g; Total Fat: 29g; Saturated Fat: 13g; Cholesterol: 91mg; Sodium: 462mg

Smoky Herb Lamb Chops and Lemon-Rosemary Dressing

SERVES: 6 | **PREP TIME:** 1 HOUR 35 MINUTES | **COOK TIME:** 10 MINUTES

Lamb chops are a great cut of meat if you know how to cook and flavor them the right way. In this dish, the lamb gets its flavor from the smoky grill and fresh herb citrus dressing. It is a very easy way to infuse the meat with flavor.

4 large cloves garlic

1 cup lemon juice

» ⅓ cup fresh rosemary

1 cup extra-virgin olive oil

1½ teaspoons salt

1 teaspoon freshly ground black pepper

» 6 1-inch-thick lamb chops

1. In a food processor or blender, blend the garlic, lemon juice, rosemary, olive oil, salt, and black pepper for 15 seconds. Set aside.

2. Put the lamb chops in a large plastic zip-top bag or container. Cover the lamb with two-thirds of the rosemary dressing, making sure that all of the lamb chops are coated with the dressing. Let the lamb marinate in the fridge for 1 hour.

3. When you are almost ready to eat, take the lamb chops out of the fridge and let them sit on the countertop for 20 minutes. Preheat a grill, grill pan, or lightly oiled skillet to high heat.

4. Cook the lamb chops for 3 minutes on each side. To serve, drizzle the lamb with the remaining dressing.

VARIATION TIP: If you don't like rosemary, you can replace it with 1 cup of fresh cilantro leaves.

PER SERVING: Calories: 484; Protein: 24g; Total Carbohydrates: 5g; Sugars: 1g; Fiber: 1g; Total Fat: 42g; Saturated Fat: 7g; Cholesterol: 73mg; Sodium: 655mg

Braised Veal

SERVES: 4 | **PREP TIME:** 10 MINUTES | **COOK TIME:** 2 HOURS

Osso buco is a popular Italian braised veal recipe very similar to this one. Everyone has their favorite version of this recipe, but the secret is being patient and letting the veal absorb all the flavors and giving it time to become tender and juicy.

» 4 veal shanks, bone in

» ½ cup flour

4 tablespoons extra-virgin olive oil

1 large onion, chopped

5 cloves garlic, sliced

2 teaspoons salt

1 tablespoon fresh thyme

» 3 tablespoons tomato paste

6 cups water

Cooked noodles, for serving (optional)

1. Preheat the oven to 350°F.

2. Dredge the veal shanks in the flour.

3. Pour the olive oil into a large oven-safe pot or pan over medium heat; add the veal shanks. Brown the veal on both sides, about 4 minutes each side. Remove the veal from pot and set aside.

4. Add the onion, garlic, salt, thyme, and tomato paste to the pan and cook for 3 to 4 minutes. Add the water, and stir to combine.

5. Add the veal back to the pan, and bring to a simmer. Cover the pan with a lid or foil and bake for 1 hour and 50 minutes. Remove from the oven and serve with cooked noodles, if desired.

VARIATION TIP: For more flavor, replace 2 cups of water with white or red wine. You can also add chopped celery and carrots to the vegetables.

PER SERVING: Calories: 400; Protein: 39g; Total Carbohydrates: 18g; Sugars: 3g; Fiber: 2g; Total Fat: 19g; Saturated Fat: 3g; Cholesterol: 143mg; Sodium: 1,368mg

Seasoned Beef Kebabs

SERVES: 6 | **PREP TIME:** 15 MINUTES | **COOK TIME:** 10 MINUTES

Beef kebabs are a traditional Mediterranean dish widely served in Greece, Turkey, and Lebanon. Fine cuts of beef deliver tender and juicy kebabs full of flavor.

» 2 pounds beef fillet

1½ teaspoons salt

1 teaspoon freshly ground black pepper

» ½ teaspoon ground allspice

» ½ teaspoon ground nutmeg

⅓ cup extra-virgin olive oil

1 large onion, cut into 8 quarters

» 1 large red bell pepper, cut into 1-inch cubes

1. Preheat a grill, grill pan, or lightly oiled skillet to high heat.

2. Cut the beef into 1-inch cubes and put them in a large bowl.

3. In a small bowl, mix together the salt, black pepper, allspice, and nutmeg.

4. Pour the olive oil over the beef and toss to coat the beef. Then evenly sprinkle the seasoning over the beef and toss to coat all pieces.

5. Skewer the beef, alternating every 1 or 2 pieces with a piece of onion or bell pepper.

6. To cook, place the skewers on the grill or skillet, and turn every 2 to 3 minutes until all sides have cooked to desired doneness, 6 minutes for medium-rare, 8 minutes for well done. Serve warm.

PREPARATION TIP: If using wood skewers, soak them in water for 5 minutes before assembling so the ends don't burn while on the grill.

PER SERVING: Calories: 485; Protein: 35g;
Total Carbohydrates: 4g; Sugars: 2g; Fiber: 1g;
Total Fat: 36g; Saturated Fat: 11g; Cholesterol: 114mg;
Sodium: 1,453mg

Grilled Skirt Steak Over Traditional Mediterranean Hummus

SERVES: 4 | **PREP TIME:** 10 MINUTES | **COOK TIME:** 10 MINUTES

This is an easy way of turning hummus into a main dish. It has extra protein from the beef and goes great with pita chips or pita bread. You can also make the hummus in advance and cook the beef just before serving.

» 1 pound skirt steak

1 teaspoon salt

½ teaspoon freshly ground black pepper

» 2 cups prepared hummus (see Creamy Traditional Hummus, page 12)

1 tablespoon extra-virgin olive oil

» ½ cup pine nuts

1. Preheat a grill, grill pan, or lightly oiled skillet to medium heat.

2. Season both sides of the steak with salt and pepper.

3. Cook the meat on each side for 3 to 5 minutes; 3 minutes for medium, and 5 minutes on each side for well done. Let the meat rest for 5 minutes.

4. Slice the meat into thin strips.

5. Spread the hummus on a serving dish, and evenly distribute the beef on top of the hummus.

6. In a small saucepan, over low heat, add the olive oil and pine nuts. Toast them for 3 minutes, constantly stirring them with a spoon so that they don't burn.

7. Spoon the pine nuts over the beef and serve.

VARIATION TIP: For added freshness, top off the dish with fresh chopped parsley. You can even add some sautéed, grilled, or caramelized onions to this.

PER SERVING: Calories: 602; Protein: 42g; Total Carbohydrates: 20g; Sugars: 1g; Fiber: 8g; Total Fat: 41g; Saturated Fat: 9g; Cholesterol: 68mg; Sodium: 1,141mg

Spanish Pepper Steak

SERVES: 4 | **PREP TIME:** 10 MINUTES | **COOK TIME:** 20 MINUTES

This is a flavorful and colorful Mediterranean spin on a classic American peppered steak. It can be served so many ways—over rice, noodles, or on a tortilla.

»1 pound beef fillet

»1 tablespoon smoked paprika

¼ cup extra-virgin olive oil

3 tablespoons garlic, minced

1½ teaspoons salt

1 large onion, sliced

»2 large bell peppers, any color, sliced

1. Cut the beef into thin strips. Season with paprika.

2. In a large skillet over medium heat, cook the olive oil, garlic, beef, and salt for 7 minutes, using tongs to toss.

3. Turn the heat to low and add in the onion. Cook for 7 minutes.

4. Add the bell peppers and cook for 6 minutes.

PREPARATION TIP: Use different colored peppers for a variety of flavors and colors. For a tangy kick, add fresh chopped cilantro leaves.

PER SERVING: Calories: 441; Protein: 28g; Total Carbohydrates: 12g; Sugars: 4g; Fiber: 3g; Total Fat: 32g; Saturated Fat: 9g; Cholesterol: 85mg; Sodium: 1,529mg

Grilled Kefta

SERVES: 4 | **PREP TIME:** 10 MINUTES | **COOK TIME:** 5 MINUTES

Kefta or kofta is ground beef or lamb that is combined with seasoning and spices. I love grilling the kefta to enhance the flavor, but it can also easily be cooked in a pan on the stovetop. Kefta goes well with a plate of hummus and a Greek salad.

1 medium onion

⅓ cup fresh Italian parsley

» 1 pound ground beef

» ¼ teaspoon ground cumin

» ¼ teaspoon cinnamon

1 teaspoon salt

½ teaspoon freshly ground black pepper

1. Preheat a grill or grill pan to high.

2. Mince the onion and parsley in a food processor until finely chopped.

3. In a large bowl, using your hands, combine the beef with the onion mix, ground cumin, cinnamon, salt, and pepper.

4. Divide the meat into 6 portions. Form each portion into a flat oval.

5. Place the patties on the grill or grill pan and cook for 3 minutes on each side.

PREPARATION TIP: You can also cook the meat in a skillet over high heat for 3 minutes on each side, making sure to keep a cover on the skillet to minimize splatter.

PER SERVING: Calories: 203; Protein: 24g; Total Carbohydrates: 3g; Sugars: 1g; Fiber: 1g; Total Fat: 10g; Saturated Fat: 4g; Cholesterol: 70mg; Sodium: 655mg

Tahini Beef and Potatoes

SERVES: 4 TO 6 | **PREP TIME:** 10 MINUTES | **COOK TIME:** 30 MINUTES

This Mediterranean version of meat and potatoes is served in a flavorful tahini sauce and is guaranteed to fill you up. The best part is you don't have to spend hours over a hot oven to make this hearty meal.

» 1 pound ground beef

2 teaspoons salt, divided

½ teaspoon freshly ground black pepper

1 large onion, finely chopped

» 10 medium golden potatoes

2 tablespoons extra-virgin olive oil

» 3 cups Greek yogurt

» 1 cup tahini

3 cloves garlic, minced

2 cups water

1. Preheat the oven to 450°F.

2. In a large bowl, using your hands, combine the beef with 1 teaspoon salt, black pepper, and the onion.

3. Form meatballs of medium size (about 1-inch), using about 2 tablespoons of the beef mixture. Place them in a deep 8-by-8-inch casserole dish.

4. Cut the potatoes into ¼-inch-thick slices. Toss them with the olive oil.

5. Lay the potato slices flat on a lined baking sheet.

6. Put the baking sheet with the potatoes and the casserole dish with the meatballs in the oven and bake for 20 minutes.

7. In a large bowl, mix together the yogurt, tahini, garlic, remaining 1 teaspoon salt, and water; set aside.

8. Once you take the meatballs and potatoes out of the oven, use a spatula to transfer the potatoes from the baking sheet to the casserole dish with the meatballs, and leave the beef drippings in the casserole dish for added flavor.

9. Reduce the oven temperature to 375°F and pour the yogurt tahini sauce over the beef and potatoes. Return it to the oven for 10 minutes. Once baking is complete, serve warm with a side of rice or pita bread.

VARIATION TIP: Top with toasted pine nuts or almond slivers once baking is complete for added crunch and flavor.

PER SERVING: Calories: 1,078; Protein: 58g; Total Carbohydrates: 89g; Sugars: 12g; Fiber: 11g; Total Fat: 59g; Saturated Fat: 14g; Cholesterol: 94mg; Sodium: 1,368mg

WHITEFISH WITH LEMON AND CAPERS,
PAGE 114

CHAPTER 8

Fish and Seafood

For me, fish and seafood recipes are some of the most important for any Mediterranean meal because the Mediterranean Sea is the focal point of the region. The fish that are harvested from the sea play an important role in what people from the Mediterranean region eat. Seafood serves as an important and healthy source of protein that seems almost endless in abundance. Cooking seafood is simple and fast—combining the right ingredients gives you a quick, flavorful, healthy dish.

Mediterranean Grilled Shrimp

SERVES: 4 TO 6 | **PREP TIME:** 20 MINUTES | **COOK TIME:** 5 MINUTES

This recipe is a surefire party pleaser! The garlic and fresh herbs pack the shrimp full of flavor that all of your guests can enjoy. Because it's cooked on a skewer, it's easy to bring to a cookout or potluck. To save time, you can marinate it in advance and grill right before serving.

2 tablespoons garlic, minced

½ cup lemon juice

3 tablespoons fresh Italian parsley, finely chopped

¼ cup extra-virgin olive oil

1 teaspoon salt

» 2 pounds jumbo shrimp (21-25), peeled and deveined

1. In a large bowl, mix the garlic, lemon juice, parsley, olive oil, and salt.

2. Add the shrimp to the bowl and toss to make sure all the pieces are coated with the marinade. Let the shrimp sit for 15 minutes.

3. Preheat a grill, grill pan, or lightly oiled skillet to high heat. While heating, thread about 5 to 6 pieces of shrimp onto each skewer.

4. Place the skewers on the grill, grill pan, or skillet and cook for 2 to 3 minutes on each side until cooked through. Serve warm.

VARIATION TIP: For added color and flavor, add 1 teaspoon paprika to the marinade.

PER SERVING: Calories: 402; Protein: 57g; Total Carbohydrates: 4g; Sugars: 1g; Fiber: 0g; Total Fat: 18g; Saturated Fat: 2g; Cholesterol: 453mg; Sodium: 1,224mg

Garlic-Cilantro Shrimp

SERVES: 4 | **PREP TIME:** 20 MINUTES | **COOK TIME:** 10 MINUTES

This shrimp recipe is super easy to make—and so delicious! It is packed full of fresh flavor from the lemon juice, garlic, and herbs. It pairs well with so many different sides—rice, pasta, mashed potatoes, or even a salad.

⅓ cup lemon juice

4 garlic cloves

» 1 cup fresh cilantro leaves

» ½ teaspoon ground coriander

3 tablespoons extra-virgin olive oil

1 teaspoon salt

» 1½ pounds large shrimp (21-25), deveined and shells removed

1. In a food processor, pulse the lemon juice, garlic, cilantro, coriander, olive oil, and salt 10 times.

2. Put the shrimp in a bowl or plastic zip-top bag, pour in the cilantro marinade, and let sit for 15 minutes.

3. Preheat a skillet on high heat.

4. Put the shrimp and marinade in the skillet. Cook the shrimp for 3 minutes on each side. Serve warm.

VARIATION TIP: Serve this dish with some buttered pasta, noodles, or rice.

PER SERVING: Calories: 225; Protein: 28g; Total Carbohydrates: 5g; Sugars: 1g; Fiber: 1g; Total Fat: 12g; Saturated Fat: 2g; Cholesterol: 218mg; Sodium: 763mg

Italian Breaded Shrimp

SERVES: 4 | **PREP TIME:** 10 MINUTES | **COOK TIME:** 5 MINUTES

This recipe is great if you're craving fried food but want to avoid the greasiness of deep-fried food. The herbs in the breading give the shrimp a mild flavor and a satisfying crunch.

» 2 large eggs

» 2 cups seasoned Italian breadcrumbs

1 teaspoon salt

» 1 cup flour

» 1 pound large shrimp (21-25), peeled and deveined

Extra-virgin olive oil

1. In a small bowl, beat the eggs with 1 tablespoon water, then transfer to a shallow dish.

2. Add the breadcrumbs and salt to a separate shallow dish; mix well.

3. Place the flour into a third shallow dish.

4. Coat the shrimp in the flour, then egg, and finally the breadcrumbs. Place on a plate and repeat with all of the shrimp.

5. Preheat a skillet over high heat. Pour in enough olive oil to coat the bottom of the skillet. Cook the shrimp in the hot skillet for 2 to 3 minutes on each side. Take the shrimp out and drain on a paper towel. Serve warm.

VARIATION TIP: Sprinkle the shrimp with freshly grated Parmesan cheese immediately after you take them out of the skillet; serve with warm marinara sauce for dipping.

PER SERVING: Calories: 714; Protein: 37g; Total Carbohydrates: 63g; Sugars: 4g; Fiber: 3g; Total Fat: 34g; Saturated Fat: 4g; Cholesterol: 243mg; Sodium: 1,727mg

Fried Fresh Sardines

SERVES: 4 | **PREP TIME:** 5 MINUTES | **COOK TIME:** 5 MINUTES

Frying fish is a great way to prepare it. You end up with a lot of flavor with very few ingredients. The fish stays flaky inside and there is a beautiful golden crunch on the outside. It is important to use fresh—not canned—sardines in this recipe. You can buy fresh-caught sardines at your local fish market and have them remove any scales.

» Avocado oil

» 1½ pounds whole fresh sardines, scales removed

1 teaspoon salt

1 teaspoon freshly ground black pepper

» 2 cups flour

1. Preheat a deep skillet over medium heat. Pour in enough oil so there is about 1 inch of it in the pan.

2. Season the fish with the salt and pepper.

3. Dredge the fish in the flour so it is completely covered.

4. Slowly drop in 1 fish at a time, making sure not to overcrowd the pan.

5. Cook for about 3 minutes on each side or just until the fish begins to brown on all sides. Serve warm.

VARIATION TIP: Serve the fish with lemon wedges and either a side of French fries or rice. Top with fresh chopped parsley for more color.

PER SERVING: Calories: 794; Protein: 48g; Total Carbohydrates: 44g; Sugars: 0g; Fiber: 2g; Total Fat: 47g; Saturated Fat: 6g; Cholesterol: 242mg; Sodium: 1,441mg

White Wine–Sautéed Mussels

SERVES: 4 | **PREP TIME:** 10 MINUTES | **COOK TIME:** 10 MINUTES

Mussels have a distinct flavor and are quite fun to eat. Dipping the salty meat of the mussel in the garlicky butter sauce with a nice crusty piece of bread makes for a fun dinner party dish.

» 3 pounds live mussels, cleaned

» 4 tablespoons (½ stick) salted butter

» 2 shallots, finely chopped

2 tablespoons garlic, minced

» 2 cups dry white wine

1. Scrub the mussel shells to make sure they are clean; trim off any that have a beard (hanging string). Put the mussels in a large bowl of water, discarding any that are not tightly closed.

2. In a large pot over medium heat, cook the butter, shallots, and garlic for 2 minutes.

3. Add the wine to the pot, and cook for 1 minute.

4. Add the mussels to the pot, toss with the sauce, and cover with a lid. Let cook for 7 minutes. Discard any mussels that have not opened.

5. Serve in bowls with the wine broth.

VARIATION TIP: Add some freshly chopped parsley, basil, or other flavorful herbs to the sauce while cooking.

PER SERVING: Calories: 777; Protein: 82g; Total Carbohydrates: 29g; Sugars: 1g; Fiber: 0g; Total Fat: 27g; Saturated Fat: 10g; Cholesterol: 221mg; Sodium: 1,344mg

Baked Swordfish with Herbs

SERVES: 4 | **PREP TIME:** 10 MINUTES | **COOK TIME:** 20 MINUTES

This is a very light dish that is great for a weeknight meal or quick lunch. The flaky swordfish and fresh herbs satisfy your hunger and go great with a green salad or wild rice.

Olive oil spray

1 cup fresh Italian parsley

¼ cup fresh thyme

¼ cup lemon juice

2 cloves garlic

¼ cup extra-virgin olive oil

½ teaspoon salt

» 4 swordfish steaks (each 5 to 7 ounces)

1. Preheat the oven to 450°F. Coat a large baking dish with olive oil spray.

2. In a food processor, pulse the parsley, thyme, lemon juice, garlic, olive oil, and salt 10 times.

3. Place the swordfish in the prepared baking dish. Spoon the parsley mixture over the steaks.

4. Put the fish in the oven to bake for 17 to 20 minutes.

VARIATION TIP: If you do not like parsley or want a bolder flavor, replace the parsley with fresh basil or cilantro. This dish also pairs well with a cherry tomato salad.

PER SERVING: Calories: 397; Protein: 44g; Total Carbohydrates: 3g; Sugars: 1g; Fiber: 1g; Total Fat: 22g; Saturated Fat: 4g; Cholesterol: 85mg; Sodium: 495mg

Grilled Sea Bass with Tahini Sauce

SERVES: 6 | **PREP TIME:** 10 MINUTES | **COOK TIME:** 10 MINUTES

Sea bass is a firm, white fish that's native to the Mediterranean region. Its mild flavor makes it a great candidate for flavorful sauces like this tahini sauce, which has a nutty flavor from the ground sesame seeds and citrus notes from the lemon juice.

» 2 pounds sea bass

Extra-virgin olive oil

» 1 cup tahini paste

1 tablespoon garlic, minced

1 teaspoon salt

⅓ cup lemon juice

1 cup water

1. Preheat a grill, grill pan, or lightly oiled skillet to medium-high heat.

2. To prepare the sea bass, pat it dry with a paper towel and brush both sides with olive oil. You can also use olive oil spray to save time.

3. In a small bowl, whisk together the tahini, garlic, salt, and lemon juice. This will become very thick. Slowly add the water (about 1 cup) until you get to your desired consistency.

4. Place the sea bass on the grill or skillet; do not move it for 6 minutes. Flip the seabass over using a spatula and cook for another 7 minutes.

5. Put the sea bass onto a plate, and drizzle with the tahini sauce. Serve with extra sauce on the side.

VARIATION TIP: Garnish with fresh chopped parsley and sliced radish.

PER SERVING: Calories: 431; Protein: 43g; Total Carbohydrates: 10g; Sugars: 1g; Fiber: 4g; Total Fat: 25g; Saturated Fat: 4g; Cholesterol: 80mg; Sodium: 565mg

Paprika-Spiced Fish

SERVES: 4 | **PREP TIME:** 5 MINUTES | **COOK TIME:** 10 MINUTES

The robust flavor of smoked paprika pairs well with the mild flavor of the sea bass. A quick pan fry gives the seasoned sea bass a thin crust and flaky texture.

» 4 (5-ounce) sea bass fillets

½ teaspoon salt

» 1 tablespoon smoked paprika

» 3 tablespoons unsalted butter

» Lemon wedges

1. Season the fish on both sides with the salt. Repeat with the paprika.

2. Preheat a skillet over high heat. Melt the butter.

3. Once the butter is melted, add the fish and cook for 4 minutes on each side.

4. Once the fish is done cooking, move to a serving dish and squeeze lemon over the top.

SUBSTITUTION TIP: Halibut can be substituted for the sea bass.

PER SERVING: Calories: 257; Protein: 34; Total Carbohydrates: 1g; Sugars: 0g; Fiber: 1g; Total Fat: 13g; Saturated Fat: 6g; Cholesterol: 98mg; Sodium: 416mg

Baked Halibut with Cherry Tomatoes

SERVES: 4 | **PREP TIME:** 5 MINUTES | **COOK TIME:** 15 MINUTES

This is a great weeknight recipe because everything is in one dish—you don't have to make a separate sauce for the fish. The tomatoes add a burst of sweet flavor.

» 4 (5-ounce) pieces of boneless halibut, skin on

» 1 pint (2 cups) cherry tomatoes

3 tablespoons garlic, minced

½ cup lemon juice

¼ cup extra-virgin olive oil

1 teaspoon salt

1. Preheat the oven to 425°F.

2. Put the halibut in a large baking dish; place the tomatoes around the halibut.

3. In a small bowl, combine the garlic, lemon juice, olive oil, and salt.

4. Pour the sauce over the halibut and tomatoes. Put the baking dish in the oven and bake for 15 minutes. Serve immediately.

VARIATION TIP: Add 1 teaspoon lemon zest and fresh chopped parsley to the sauce.

PER SERVING: Calories: 350; Protein: 39g; Total Carbohydrates: 8g; Sugars: 3g; Fiber: 1g; Total Fat: 18g; Saturated Fat: 3g; Cholesterol: 58mg; Sodium: 687mg

Grilled Salmon

SERVES: 4 | **PREP TIME:** 5 MINUTES | **COOK TIME:** 10 MINUTES

Grilling is a great way to cook seafood because it adds a smoky flavor. Salmon is an especially good fish for grilling because its natural fat content keeps the fish nice and moist. When grilled, salmon cooks up nice and flaky with a crispy skin.

» 1 teaspoon garlic powder

» 1 teaspoon onion powder

1 teaspoon freshly ground black pepper

½ teaspoon salt

» 4 (5- to 6-ounce) salmon fillets with skin on

½ cup lemon juice

1. In a small bowl, mix together the garlic powder, onion powder, black pepper, and salt.

2. Put the salmon in a large dish; pour the lemon juice over the salmon.

3. Season the salmon with the seasoning mix.

4. Preheat a grill, grill pan, or lightly oiled skillet to high heat. Place the salmon on the grill or skillet, skin-side down first.

5. Cook each side for 4 minutes. Serve immediately.

PREPARATION TIP: To enhance the flavors, you can marinate the salmon in the lemon juice and seasoning a few hours before cooking.

PER SERVING: Calories: 238; Protein: 29g; Total Carbohydrates: 4g; Sugars: 1g; Fiber: 0g; Total Fat: 13g; Saturated Fat: 3g; Cholesterol: 56mg; Sodium: 360mg

Baked Salmon and Tomato Pockets

SERVES: 4 | **PREP TIME:** 5 MINUTES | **COOK TIME:** 25 MINUTES

This is a fun dish to serve for a dinner because each person gets their own pocket of fish to open. The acidic flavor of the tomatoes cuts through the fatty salmon, while the oregano gives the dish an earthy flavor.

» 1 pint (2 cups) cherry tomatoes

3 tablespoons extra-virgin olive oil

3 tablespoons lemon juice

» 1 teaspoon oregano

» 3 tablespoons unsalted butter, melted

½ teaspoon salt

» 4 (5-ounce) salmon fillets

1. Preheat the oven to 400°F.

2. Cut the tomatoes in half and put them in a bowl.

3. Add the olive oil, lemon juice, oregano, melted butter, and salt to the tomatoes and toss to combine.

4. Cut 4 pieces of foil, about 12-by-12 inches each.

5. Place the salmon in the middle of each piece of foil.

6. Divide the tomato mixture evenly over the 4 pieces of salmon. Bring the ends of the foil together and seal to form a closed pocket.

7. Place the 4 pockets on a baking sheet. Cook for 25 minutes.

8. To serve, place each pocket on a plate and let your guests open to reveal the baked salmon and tomatoes.

VARIATION TIP: Try adding different veggies to the pockets, such as asparagus or cut green beans.

PER SERVING: Calories: 410; Protein: 30g; Total Carbohydrates: 4g; Sugars: 2g; Fiber: 1g; Total Fat: 32g; Saturated Fat: 9g; Cholesterol: 80mg; Sodium: 370mg

Balsamic-Glazed Salmon

SERVES: 4 | **PREP TIME:** 10 MINUTES | **COOK TIME:** 25 MINUTES

Balsamic glaze is an easy way to really enliven a piece of fish or poultry. The glaze's sweet but tangy flavor complements any fish or white meat. In this recipe, the taste of the glaze cuts through the fishy salmon to balance out the flavors.

» ½ cup balsamic vinegar

» 2 tablespoons honey

1 teaspoon garlic, minced

» 4 (5-ounce) salmon fillets, skin on

½ teaspoon salt

Freshly ground black pepper

1. Preheat the oven to 400°F.

2. In a saucepan over medium heat, cook the vinegar, honey, and garlic, stirring, for 5 to 7 minutes or until the glaze begins to thicken. Remove from heat.

3. Season the salmon with salt and pepper. Place in a baking dish, skin-side down. Brush the salmon with the balsamic glaze. Reserve remainder of the glaze.

4. Put the salmon in the oven and bake for 20 minutes.

5. Remove the salmon from the oven and spoon the remainder of the glaze over the top of the salmon. Serve warm with freshly ground black pepper.

VARIATION TIP: For some kick, add 1 tablespoon of spicy mustard to the glaze when it's cooking.

PER SERVING: Calories: 274; Protein: 29g; Total Carbohydrates: 13g; Sugars: 9g; Fiber: 0g; Total Fat: 13g; Saturated Fat: 3g; Cholesterol: 56mg; Sodium: 370mg

Whitefish with Lemon and Capers

SERVES: 4 | **PREP TIME:** 5 MINUTES | **COOK TIME:** 20 MINUTES

This is an easy fish recipe that you can whip up in a pinch. The highlight of this recipe is the flavorful sauce. The capers give the fish a briny flavor while the butter gives it a subtle sweetness.

» 4 (4- to 5-ounce) cod fillets (or any whitefish)

1 tablespoon extra-virgin olive oil

1 teaspoon salt, divided

» 4 tablespoons (½ stick) unsalted butter

» 2 tablespoons capers, drained

3 tablespoons lemon juice

½ teaspoon freshly ground black pepper

1. Preheat the oven to 450°F. Put the cod in a large baking dish and drizzle with the olive oil and ½ teaspoon of salt. Bake for 15 minutes.

2. Right before the fish is done cooking, melt the butter in a small saucepan over medium heat. Add the capers, lemon juice, remaining ½ teaspoon of salt, and pepper; simmer for 30 seconds.

3. Place the fish in a serving dish once it is done baking; spoon the caper sauce over the fish and serve.

VARIATION TIP: For an extra punch of lemon flavor, add 1 teaspoon lemon zest to the sauce while it is cooking. Sprinkle fresh chopped parsley or dill onto the dish for additional flavor.

PER SERVING: Calories: 255; Protein: 26g; Total Carbohydrates: 1g; Sugars: 0g; Fiber: 0g; Total Fat: 16g; Saturated Fat: 8g; Cholesterol: 94mg; Sodium: 801mg

Saffron Rice with Whitefish

SERVES: 4 | **PREP TIME:** 10 MINUTES | **COOK TIME:** 35 MINUTES

Saffron is a very common ingredient in Spanish cuisine. It adds a warm, earthy flavor and color and is frequently used in rice dishes. This bold spice pairs well with the subtle flavors of the whitefish.

4 tablespoons extra-virgin olive oil, divided

1 large onion, chopped

» 3 cod fillets, rinsed and patted dry

4½ cups water

» 1 teaspoon saffron threads

1½ teaspoons salt

» 1 teaspoon turmeric

» 2 cups long-grain rice, rinsed

1. In a large pot over medium heat, cook 2 tablespoons of olive oil and the onions for 5 minutes.

2. While the onions are cooking, preheat another large pan over high heat. Add the remaining 2 tablespoons of olive oil and the cod fillets. Cook the cod for 2 minutes on each side, then remove from the pan and set aside.

3. Once the onions are done cooking, add the water, saffron, salt, turmeric, and rice, stirring to combine. Cover and cook for 12 minutes.

4. Cut the cod up into 1-inch pieces. Place the cod pieces in the rice, lightly toss, cover, and cook for another 10 minutes.

5. Once the rice is done cooking, fluff with a fork, cover, and let stand for 5 minutes. Serve warm.

PREPARATION TIP: Cod is usually readily available. If you cannot find it fresh, frozen cod is fine. Defrost the fish by placing it in the fridge the night before; this should easily and safely thaw the fish in time for dinner.

PER SERVING: Calories: 564; Protein: 26g; Total Carbohydrates: 78g; Sugars: 2g; Fiber: 2g; Total Fat: 15g; Saturated Fat: 2g; Cholesterol: 47mg; Sodium: 945mg

Roasted Red Snapper

SERVES: 4 | **PREP TIME:** 5 MINUTES | **COOK TIME:** 45 MINUTES

Red snapper is a lean, moist, and flaky whitefish with a mildly sweet flavor. It is a great fish for roasting and does well when adding a robust herb flavor. The red skin of the snapper and the yellow lemon slices make for a pretty presentation.

» 1 (2 to 2½ pounds) whole red snapper, cleaned and scaled

» 2 lemons, sliced (about 10 slices)

3 cloves garlic, sliced

4 or 5 sprigs of thyme

» 3 tablespoons cold salted butter, cut into small cubes, divided

1. Preheat the oven to 350°F.

2. Cut a piece of foil to about the size of your baking sheet; put the foil on the baking sheet.

3. Make a horizontal slice through the belly of the fish to create a pocket.

4. Place 3 slices of lemon on the foil and the fish on top of the lemons.

5. Stuff the fish with the garlic, thyme, 3 lemon slices and butter. Reserve 3 pieces of butter.

6. Place the reserved 3 pieces of butter on top of the fish, and 3 or 4 slices of lemon on top of the butter. Bring the foil together and seal it to make a pocket around the fish.

7. Put the fish in the oven and bake for 45 minutes. Serve with remaining fresh lemon slices.

PREPARATION TIP: The fish can be assembled in the foil ahead of time and placed in the fridge until you are ready to bake it. Remove the fish from the fridge and let it sit out for 10 minutes before baking.

PER SERVING: Calories: 345; Protein: 54g; Total Carbohydrates: 12g; Sugars: 0g; Fiber: 3g; Total Fat: 13g; Saturated Fat: 6g; Cholesterol: 103mg; Sodium: 170mg

Pan-Fried Cod

SERVES: 4 | **PREP TIME:** 5 MINUTES | **COOK TIME:** 10 MINUTES

Cod is very mild, so this is a good recipe for picky fish eaters. The light breading makes it great for a sandwich or to serve with French fries. This recipe gives you the flavor of fish and chips without the greasiness.

»½ cup flour

1 teaspoon salt

»1 teaspoon garlic powder

»4 (4- to 5-ounce) cod fillets

»3 tablespoons herb butter, either purchased or homemade (see recipe this page)

1. In a shallow plate combine the flour, salt, and garlic powder.

2. Dredge the cod fillets in the seasoned flour until they are completely coated.

3. Preheat a medium pan over medium-high heat. Melt the herb butter.

4. Once the butter has melted, add the cod fillets to the pan and cook for 3 to 4 minutes on each side.

5. Remove from the pan and serve as part of a sandwich or with French fries.

VARIATION TIP: You can season the flour with any spices or herbs that you like: onion powder, oregano, paprika, freshly ground black pepper, marjoram, or even tarragon. For a lighter meal, serve with rice or a salad.

TO MAKE HERB BUTTER: Combine 1 stick of room-temperature butter with 1 teaspoon minced garlic, 1 tablespoon fresh chopped parsley, and 1 tablespoon fresh basil.

PER SERVING: Calories: 248; Protein: 27g; Total Carbohydrates: 12g; Sugars: 0g; Fiber: 1g; Total Fat: 10g; Saturated Fat: 6g; Cholesterol: 86mg; Sodium: 671mg

Seafood Risotto

SERVES: 4 | **PREP TIME:** 10 MINUTES | **COOK TIME:** 30 MINUTES

Seafood is very common in Mediterranean cuisine because of the proximity to the Mediterranean Sea. This recipe uses shrimp and scallops, which are both fairly easy to prepare and found in almost any market.

» 6 cups vegetable broth

3 tablespoons extra-virgin olive oil

1 large onion, chopped

3 cloves garlic, minced

» ½ teaspoon saffron threads

» 1½ cups arborio rice

1½ teaspoons salt

» 8 ounces shrimp (21-25), peeled and deveined

» 8 ounces scallops

1. In a large saucepan over medium heat, bring the broth to a low simmer.

2. In a large skillet over medium heat, cook the olive oil, onion, garlic, and saffron for 3 minutes.

3. Add the rice, salt, and 1 cup of the broth to the skillet. Stir the ingredients together and cook over low heat until most of the liquid is absorbed. Repeat steps with broth, adding ½ cup of broth at a time, and cook until all but ½ cup of the broth is absorbed.

4. Add the shrimp and scallops when you stir in the final ½ cup of broth. Cover and let cook for 10 minutes. Serve warm.

VARIATION TIP: To give the dish a zesty fresh flavor, add a squeeze of lemon and a sprinkle of freshly chopped parsley when you are ready to serve. Garnish with additional lemon wedges.

PER SERVING: Calories: 460; Protein: 24g; Total Carbohydrates: 64g; Sugars: 5g; Fiber: 2g; Total Fat: 12g; Saturated Fat: 2g; Cholesterol: 91mg; Sodium: 2,432mg

MINTY WATERMELON SALAD, PAGE 122

CHAPTER 9

Sweets and Desserts

Desserts and sweets are always a great way to end a meal. Whether the sweet is a decadent cheesecake or a crumbly cookie with a cup of tea, desserts are made to satisfy a sweet tooth. Many of these desserts incorporate nuts or native fruits like figs and dates. They are definitely more rustic in nature but have a simple elegance. These recipes don't have to be served just at dinner; they can be great for an afternoon coffee or tea or even served with breakfast. It's never a bad idea to have something sweet as a pick-me-up!

Minty Watermelon Salad

SERVES: 6 TO 8 | **PREP TIME:** 10 MINUTES

This dessert salad immediately brings feelings of warm summer days spent enjoying a fresh breeze. It satisfies your sweet tooth with the refreshing flavor of the watermelon and minty dressing, without needing to fuss with an oven or baking.

» 1 medium watermelon

» 1 cup fresh blueberries

» 2 tablespoons fresh mint leaves

2 tablespoons lemon juice

» ⅓ cup honey

1. Cut the watermelon into 1-inch cubes. Put them in a bowl.

2. Evenly distribute the blueberries over the watermelon.

3. Finely chop the mint leaves and put them into a separate bowl.

4. Add the lemon juice and honey to the mint and whisk together.

5. Drizzle the mint dressing over the watermelon and blueberries. Serve cold.

VARIATION TIP: Add ½ cup crumbled feta cheese to this salad for a salty twist.

PER SERVING: Calories: 238; Protein: 4g; Total Carbohydrates: 61g; Sugars: 52g; Fiber: 3g; Total Fat: 1g; Saturated Fat: 0g; Cholesterol: 0mg; Sodium: 11mg

Mascarpone and Fig Crostini

SERVES: 6 TO 8 | **PREP TIME:** 10 MINUTES | **COOK TIME:** 10 MINUTES

This easy recipe involves minimal baking but results in an elegant dessert that is creamy, crunchy, and sweet. When you serve this, you'll be able to spend your time with your guests instead of in the kitchen.

» 1 long French baguette

» 4 tablespoons (½ stick) salted butter, melted

» 1 (8-ounce) tub mascarpone cheese

» 1 (12-ounce) jar fig jam or preserves

1. Preheat the oven to 350°F.

2. Slice the bread into ¼-inch-thick slices.

3. Arrange the sliced bread on a baking sheet and brush each slice with the melted butter.

4. Put the baking sheet in the oven and toast the bread for 5 to 7 minutes, just until golden brown.

5. Let the bread cool slightly. Spread about a teaspoon or so of the mascarpone cheese on each piece of bread.

6. Top with a teaspoon or so of the jam. Serve immediately.

SUBSTITUTION TIP: You can substitute the fig jam with apricot jam or preserves.

PER SERVING: Calories: 445; Protein: 3g; Total Carbohydrates: 48g; Sugars: 24g; Fiber: 5g; Total Fat: 24g; Saturated Fat: 12g; Cholesterol: 74mg; Sodium: 314mg

Crunchy Sesame Cookies

YIELD: 14 TO 16 | **PREP TIME:** 10 MINUTES | **COOK TIME:** 15 MINUTES

The nutty flavor of the sesame seeds makes these cookies a great treat to serve with afternoon tea or coffee. Their crunchy texture makes them perfect for dipping!

» 1 cup sesame seeds, hulled

» 1 cup sugar

» 8 tablespoons (1 stick) salted butter, softened

» 2 large eggs

» 1¼ cups flour

1. Preheat the oven to 350°F. Toast the sesame seeds on a baking sheet for 3 minutes. Set aside and let cool.

2. Using a mixer, cream together the sugar and butter.

3. Add the eggs one at a time until well-blended.

4. Add the flour and toasted sesame seeds and mix until well-blended.

5. Drop spoonfuls of cookie dough onto a baking sheet and form them into round balls, about 1-inch in diameter, similar to a walnut.

6. Put in the oven and bake for 5 to 7 minutes or until golden brown.

7. Let the cookies cool and enjoy.

VARIATION TIP: You can add ½ teaspoon of cinnamon to the cookie mix for a nice added flavor.

PER SERVING: Calories: 218; Protein: 4g; Total Carbohydrates: 25g; Sugars: 14g; Fiber: 2g; Total Fat: 12g; Saturated Fat: 5g; Cholesterol: 44mg; Sodium: 58mg

Almond Cookies

SERVES: 4 TO 6, ABOUT 2 DOZEN COOKIES | **PREP TIME:** 5 MINUTES
COOK TIME: 10 MINUTES

This is a great recipe for people who love almonds! It's full of nutty almond flavor but not too sweet. This cookie has a soft crunch and goes great with a hot mug of Earl Grey tea.

» ½ cup sugar

» 8 tablespoons (1 stick) room temperature salted butter

» 1 large egg

» 1½ cups all-purpose flour

» 1 cup ground almonds or almond flour

1. Preheat the oven to 375°F.

2. Using a mixer, cream together the sugar and butter.

3. Add the egg and mix until combined.

4. Alternately add the flour and ground almonds, ½ cup at a time, while the mixer is on slow.

5. Once everything is combined, line a baking sheet with parchment paper. Drop a tablespoon of dough on the baking sheet, keeping the cookies at least 2 inches apart.

6. Put the baking sheet in the oven and bake just until the cookies start to turn brown around the edges, about 5 to 7 minutes.

PREPARATION TIP: You can make the dough ahead and keep in the fridge for a day and bake the cookies right before serving. This recipe can be used as a base for more ingredients, such as sliced almonds for more crunch or a teaspoon of vanilla or vanilla paste for more flavor.

PER SERVING: Calories: 604; Protein: 11g; Total Carbohydrates: 63g; Sugars: 26g; Fiber: 4g; Total Fat: 36g; Saturated Fat: 16g; Cholesterol: 108mg; Sodium: 181mg

Baklava and Honey

SERVES: 6 TO 8 | **PREP TIME:** 40 MINUTES | **COOK TIME:** 1 HOUR

There are so many baklava variations; personally, I've tried at least 10. This recipe takes the traditional approach with simple ingredients and easy layering, resulting in a nice sweet-sticky piece of crunchy baklava without the hassle.

» 2 cups very finely chopped walnuts or pecans

» 1 teaspoon cinnamon

» 1 cup (2 sticks) of unsalted butter, melted

» 1 (16-ounce) package phyllo dough, thawed

» 1 (12-ounce) jar honey

1. Preheat the oven to 350°F.

2. In a bowl, combine the chopped nuts and cinnamon.

3. Using a brush, butter the sides and bottom of a 9-by-13-inch inch baking dish.

4. Remove the phyllo dough from the package and cut it to the size of the baking dish using a sharp knife.

5. Place one sheet of phyllo dough on the bottom of the dish, brush with butter, and repeat until you have 8 layers.

6. Sprinkle ⅓ cup of the nut mixture over the phyllo layers. Top with a sheet of phyllo dough, butter that sheet, and repeat until you have 4 sheets of buttered phyllo dough.

7. Sprinkle ⅓ cup of the nut mixture for another layer of nuts. Repeat the layering of nuts and 4 sheets of buttered phyllo until all the nut mixture is gone. The last layer should be 8 buttered sheets of phyllo.

8. Before you bake, cut the baklava into desired shapes; traditionally this is diamonds, triangles, or squares.

9. Bake the baklava for 1 hour or until the top layer is golden brown.

10. While the baklava is baking, heat the honey in a pan just until it is warm and easy to pour.

11. Once the baklava is done baking, immediately pour the honey evenly over the baklava and let it absorb it, about 20 minutes. Serve warm or at room temperature.

VARIATION TIP: For those who cannot have honey, use a simple syrup instead. Combine 2 parts sugar to 1 part water. You can add a squeeze of lemon juice to it and 1 tablespoon each of rose water and orange blossom water. You can also add the orange blossom water and rose water to the nut mixture for even more flavor.

PER SERVING: Calories: 1,235; Protein: 18g; Total Carbohydrates: 109g; Sugars: 60g; Fiber: 7g; Total Fat: 89g; Saturated Fat: 25g; Cholesterol: 83mg; Sodium: 588mg

Date and Nut Balls

SERVES: 6 TO 8 | **PREP TIME:** 10 MINUTES | **COOK TIME:** 10 MINUTES

This is not only a dessert but an energy ball. The natural sweetness of the dates with the nutrient-packed nuts and coconut make for a great-tasting snack for both kids and adults.

» 1 cup walnuts
   or pistachios

» 1 cup unsweetened
   shredded coconut

» 14 medjool dates,
   pits removed

» 8 tablespoons (1 stick)
   butter, melted

1. Preheat the oven to 350°F.

2. Put the nuts on a baking sheet. Toast the nuts for 5 minutes.

3. Put the shredded coconut on a clean baking sheet; toast just until it turns golden brown, about 3 to 5 minutes (coconut burns fast so keep an eye on it). Once done, remove it from the oven and put it in a shallow bowl.

4. In a food processor fitted with a chopping blade, process the nuts until they have a medium chop. Put the chopped nuts into a medium bowl.

5. Add the dates and melted butter to the food processor and blend until the dates become a thick paste. Pour the chopped nuts into the food processor with the dates and pulse just until the mixture is combined, about 5 to 7 pulses.

6. Remove the mixture from the food processor and scrape it into a large bowl.

7. To make the balls, spoon 1 to 2 tablespoons of the date mixture into the palm of your hand and roll around between your hands until you form a ball. Put the ball on a clean, lined baking sheet. Repeat until all the mixture is formed into balls.

8. Roll each ball in the toasted coconut until the outside of the ball is coated, put the ball back on the baking sheet, and repeat.

9. Put all the balls into the fridge for 20 minutes before serving so that they firm up. You can also store any leftovers in the fridge in an airtight container.

SUBSTITUTION TIP: You can substitute the coconut for a different type of finely chopped nut or toasted sesame seeds. Another variation is to chill the date balls and then coat them in melted chocolate.

PER SERVING: Calories: 489; Protein: 5g; Total Carbohydrates: 48g; Sugars: 39g; Fiber: 7g; Total Fat: 35g; Saturated Fat: 19g; Cholesterol: 41mg; Sodium: 114mg

Creamy Rice Pudding

SERVES: 6 | **PREP TIME:** 5 MINUTES | **COOK TIME:** 45 MINUTES

Because the ingredients are so easy to come by, many countries around the world have their own version of rice pudding. This version has creamy and flowery flavor, with a nice touch of spice from the cinnamon.

» 1¼ cups long-grain rice

» 5 cups whole milk

» 1 cup sugar

» 1 tablespoon rose water or orange blossom water

» 1 teaspoon cinnamon

1. Rinse the rice under cold water for 30 seconds.

2. Put the rice, milk, and sugar in a large pot. Bring to a gentle boil while continually stirring.

3. Turn the heat down to low and let simmer for 40 to 45 minutes, stirring every 3 to 4 minutes so that the rice does not stick to the bottom of the pot.

4. Add the rose water at the end and simmer for 5 minutes.

5. Divide the pudding into 6 bowls. Sprinkle the top with cinnamon. Cool for at least 1 hour before serving. Store in the fridge.

VARIATION TIP: You can also add ½ cup of golden raisins about halfway through the cooking time. Different toppings can be added as well—chopped pistachios or toasted coconut are some of my favorites.

PER SERVING: Calories: 394; Protein: 9g; Total Carbohydrates: 75g; Sugars: 43g; Fiber: 1g; Total Fat: 7g; Saturated Fat: 4g; Cholesterol: 29mg; Sodium: 102mg

Ricotta-Lemon Cheesecake

SERVES: 8 TO 10 | **PREP TIME:** 5 MINUTES | **COOK TIME:** 1 HOUR

Traditional cheesecake can be so decadent and dense. The ricotta and lemon zest in this cheesecake give it a light flavor and texture.

» 2 (8-ounce) packages full-fat cream cheese

» 1 (16-ounce) container full-fat ricotta cheese

» 1½ cups granulated sugar

» 1 tablespoon lemon zest

» 5 large eggs

Nonstick cooking spray

1. Preheat the oven to 350°F.

2. Using a mixer, blend together the cream cheese and ricotta cheese.

3. Blend in the sugar and lemon zest.

4. Blend in the eggs; drop in 1 egg at a time, blend for 10 seconds, and repeat.

5. Line a 9-inch springform pan with parchment paper and nonstick spray. Wrap the bottom of the pan with foil. Pour the cheesecake batter into the pan.

6. To make a water bath, get a baking or roasting pan larger than the cheesecake pan. Fill the roasting pan about ⅓ of the way up with warm water. Put the cheesecake pan into the water bath. Put the whole thing in the oven and let the cheesecake bake for 1 hour.

7. After baking is complete, remove the cheesecake pan from the water bath and remove the foil. Let the cheesecake cool for 1 hour on the countertop. Then put it in the fridge to cool for at least 3 hours before serving.

PREPARATION TIP: You can make the cheesecake a day or two ahead of serving. To dress up the cheesecake, top with fresh berries, such as raspberries, strawberries, blueberries, or blackberries.

PER SERVING: Calories: 489; Protein: 15g; Total Carbohydrates: 42g; Sugars: 40g; Fiber: 0g; Total Fat: 31g; Saturated Fat: 17g; Cholesterol: 210mg; Sodium: 264mg

Measurement Conversions

VOLUME EQUIVALENTS (LIQUID)

US STANDARD	US STANDARD (OUNCES)	METRIC (APPROXIMATE)
2 tablespoons	1 fl. oz.	30 mL
¼ cup	2 fl. oz.	60 mL
½ cup	4 fl. oz.	120 mL
1 cup	8 fl. oz.	240 mL
1½ cups	12 fl. oz.	355 mL
2 cups or 1 pint	16 fl. oz.	475 mL
4 cups or 1 quart	32 fl. oz.	1 L
1 gallon	128 fl. oz.	4 L

OVEN TEMPERATURES

FAHRENHEIT (F)	CELSIUS (C) (APPROXIMATE)
250°F	120°C
300°F	150°C
325°F	165°C
350°F	180°C
375°F	190°C
400°F	200°C
425°F	220°C
450°F	230°C

VOLUME EQUIVALENTS (DRY)

US STANDARD	METRIC (APPROXIMATE)
⅛ teaspoon	0.5 mL
¼ teaspoon	1 mL
½ teaspoon	2 mL
¾ teaspoon	4 mL
1 teaspoon	5 mL
1 tablespoon	15 mL
¼ cup	59 mL
⅓ cup	79 mL
½ cup	118 mL
⅔ cup	156 mL
¾ cup	177 mL
1 cup	235 mL
2 cups or 1 pint	475 mL
3 cups	700 mL
4 cups or 1 quart	1 L

WEIGHT EQUIVALENTS

US STANDARD	METRIC (APPROXIMATE)
½ ounce	15 g
1 ounce	30 g
2 ounces	60 g
4 ounces	115 g
8 ounces	225 g
12 ounces	340 g
16 ounces or 1 pound	455 g

Index

Ingredients

1.2kg red-skinned potatoes, chopped into small ch

500g undyed smoked haddock fillets

600ml whole milk

1 bay leaf

75g butter

Acknowledgments

To my beautiful and talented daughters, London and Berlin, I hope that I make you proud with this book, and I hope that one day you use and pass on this book to your families. You inspire me to keep pushing onward and upward and to be the best role model of what a strong successful mom can be. You are my love, my heart, my sunshine, and my happiness. I am so thankful that I have you two in my life.

To my husband, who encouraged me to take the chance on this food path 13 years ago. Thank you for being my cooking critic, even though sometimes I think you were wrong. Thank you for making me a better cook, chef, and artist. I love you.

I'd also like to thank my parents, sisters, and brother for supporting and encouraging me. Thanks to my mom, the best cook I have ever known, who always put so much love and effort into her cooking—you taught me so much of what I know about cooking, you let me take over your kitchen any chance I could get, and you have passed along amazing Lebanese recipes to my family. Thanks to my dad for always encouraging me and teaching me to be strong. To my brother Haidar for being the best taste tester. To my sisters, Angela and Nadeen, for being there for me no matter what was happening and for being the best sisters in the world and my best friends. And thanks to my aunts, who made cooking at family events a competition and taught me to always WOW people.

To my fans and followers throughout the years, thank you for your kind words and stories. Every single message meant so much, and I could not have moved forward without your support.

I'd like to also thank Daniel Petrino for his patience and encouraging words and for helping guide me in writing this book.

About the Author

© Leah Hardy Photography

Denise Hazime is a native Michigander currently living in California. She grew up in a large Lebanese family as the first generation born in the USA. Her love of cooking began at a young age and turned into an online presence in 2006 when she began posting cooking videos on YouTube. With 13 million views on her YouTube videos, she's known for her easy-to-follow and healthy recipes. She also has one of the most popular hummus recipes on the internet and was called the "Queen of the Smashed Chickpea" on the front page of the *Wall Street Journal*. She has also appeared on CNN, in *Coast Magazine*, and many other nationwide outlets. In 2013, she was invited to Food Network's New York City Wine and Food Festival by Hidden Valley Ranch and won the best sandwich. Her first cookbook was published in 2014.

Although her passion is cooking, she enjoys business and currently runs a tech company out of Los Angeles. She was named to Forbes' Business Development Council and has spoken at several entrepreneurship and women-in-tech events.

CPSIA information can be obtained
at www.ICGtesting.com
Printed in the USA
BVHW090830070620
581005BV00016B/1995

9 781646 111251